Fatimah

Third Edition

Islamic Studies

Level 1

Mansur Ahmad and Husain A. Nuri

Copyright © Weekend Learning Publishers, 2008, 2009

Copyright under International Pan American and Universal Copyright Conventions. All rights reserved. No parts of this book may be reproduced or transmitted in any forms or by any means, electronic, mechanical, including photocopying, recording or any information storage and retrieval system, without written permission from the copyright holder. Brief passage not exceeding 100 words may be quoted only for reviews.

No part or pages of the book may be photocopied for classroom use.

ISBN: 978-0-9818483-3-4

First edition: 2008
Second edition: 2009
Third edition: 2010

Cover Design and Photography: Mansur Ahmad
Illustrations: Mansur Ahmad, Husain A. Nuri

WeekendLearning Publishers
5584 Boulder Crest St
Columbus, OH 43235
www.weekendlearning.com

Printed in China

Preface

The concept of a series of Islamic Studies books was conceived in 2002 when both of us were teachers and/or principals of two weekend schools in two different states. We used several excellent textbooks or reference books for the schools. However, as teachers soon we realized there was no single textbook available that could meet our classroom needs. Some of the available books have too many or too few lessons for an academic year. Some lessons are too long for a class hour, some are too short. Some lessons are too difficult for the age; some are too basic for higher classes. Some books are written without a 12 year curriculum in mind. The lessons in higher grades, therefore, did not develop from the knowledge base of the prior years. Sometimes, extra emphasis was placed on one topic at the cost of other important topics. We thought a balanced knowledge base was, thus, lost.

We always felt there ought to be a way out. We began writing the lessons ourselves to meet the needs of our schools. We involved other teachers. For the next two years, we conducted classes based on the lessons we prepared. In the meantime, both of us met other principals and teachers across the country. We wanted to find out how they teach Islamic Studies and what their major concerns were. Most of the principals and teachers we talked to, expressed their inability to find or develop a good curriculum. If they had a curriculum they could not find lessons to complement the curriculum.

This survey prompted us to develop a functional, comprehensive curriculum for weekend schools in the West. We wanted to have a curriculum that would include everything Muslim students growing up in the West would ideally need to know. We wanted to include topics based on the life experiences of students growing up in the West. Muslim children growing up in the US, Europe and Australia are facing diverse challenges and conflicting pressures at schools and at friend circles. They are constantly influenced by mainstream youth culture. We wanted lessons to address their issues from their perspective.

The curriculum alone would not be of any use unless there were lessons based on the curriculum. The lessons had to be age appropriate, suitable for typical class duration of most of the schools. As we continued to write and edit lessons over the next two years, we made the curriculum increasingly meaningful.

In 2007 we published pre-printed coil bound versions of these books. More than thirty schools in the US and UK used the books. We also received large number of inquiries from many other schools. Based on the suggestions, comments and reviews received from many of these schools, we have edited the books and made changes as appropriate.

We are thankful to Allāh for giving us the ability to write these books. We pray to Allāh to accept our labor and make us successful in communicating the message of Islam. We hope Islamic schools and home schools in the USA and other countries will find these books useful. Any mistakes or errors in the books are our fault. We will appreciate receiving meaningful comments and suggestions to improve the series.

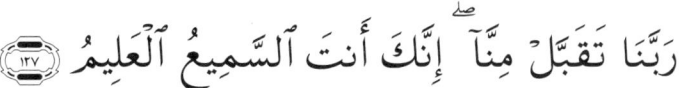

"Our Rabb! Accept from us, you indeed are the all-Hearing, all-Knowing." (2:127)

January 15, 2008   Mansur Ahmad
                                                                                              Husain A. Nuri

Preface to the Second Edition

Alhamdulillah, tne second edition of the book is now ready. Second edition gives us the scope to improve upon the text, presentation and format without sacrificing the overall ease of use and appeal of the lessons. Each lesson now has two to three self-check review questions. We hope this will help reinforce learning. The self-check questions will refresh the students to continue with the lesson. We have reformatted the homework section to make it user friendly.

We thank all the teachers and home-schooling parents for adopting this and other books in the series. We hope this edition too will receive similar recognition from weekend schools, teachers, students and parents. May Allāh accept our small effort.

February 15, 2009

Mansur Ahmad
Husain A. Nuri

Preface to the Third Edition

As the third edition of the Level 1 book became due, the first thing we did was to convert it into a color edition. We hope this will increase overall appeal of the book even more. We retained all other features of the second edition, which was hugely popular with parents, students and teachers.

As always, we thank Allāh for giving us the time, resources and ability to continue working on this and other books in this series. Our special thanks also goes out to all the teachers and home-schooling parents for adopting the book. We hope this edition too will continue receiving recognition from weekend schools, teachers, students and parents. May Allāh accept our small effort.

February 15, 2010

Mansur Ahmad
Husain A. Nuri

Table of Contents

1. Allah: *Our Creator* — 8
2. Islam — 13
3. Our Faith — 18
4. Prophet Muhammad (S) — 23
5. The Qur'an — 28
6. 5 Pillars of Islam — 33
7. Shahadah: *The First Pillar* — 38
8. Salah: *The Second Pillar* — 42
9. Fasting: *The Third Pillar* — 47
10. Zakat: *The Fourth Pillar* — 52
11. Hajj: *The Fifth Pillar* — 57
12. Saying Bismillah: *Remembering Allah* — 62
13. Angels: *They Always Work for Allah* — 67
14. Shaitan: *Our Enemy* — 72
15. Adam (A): *The First Prophet* — 77
16. Nuh (A): *Saved From The Great Flood* — 82

17. Ibrahim (A): *Never Listen to Shaitan*	87
18. Musa (A): *A Good Man Against a Bad Ruler*	92
19. Isa (A): *A Good Son of a Good Mother*	97
20. Makkah and Madinah: *Two Great Places*	102
21. Good Manners	107
22. Kindness and Sharing	112
23. Allah Rewards Good Work	117
24. Respect	122
25. Forgiveness	127
26. Love of Allah	132
27. Eid: *Two Festivals*	137
28. Thanking Allah	142

How to use this book effectively
Instructions to the teacher and parents:

Each lesson in this grade starts with a coloring or an activity page. The purpose of this page is to help the students to compose themselves before the lesson starts. Students should be given about 5-10 minutes to complete the coloring. A word of appreciation or encouragement, insha-Allāh, will improve the attention of the class. If the teacher sits close to the students, and at a similar height to the chairs of the students, s/he might be able to draw more attention. Please avoid monotonous voice; rather change the voice from loud to whispers as appropriate. Use body languages, such as, use your hands to show a flying bird when you are teaching "Allah created all the birds." Be creative in teaching!

Homework:

Teachers are requested to assign and grade homework regularly. The time commitment for homework for this grade is about 10 minutes per lesson. The homework is designed to reinforce the materials learned in the class and to develop a regular study habit.

As reading skill varies among the first graders, some students may not be able to read and understand all the instructions. It is strongly encouraged that a parent works with the student for the homework, even if the student is an excellent reader. A regular supervision by a parent of homework will indicate the education is valued. Most of the homework in first grade require minimum amount of writing.

Teaching Respect:

From an early age, students should be taught to show respect to Allāh, His Prophets, Angels and the Companions. The teachers and parents are requested to mention the following:

- Whenever the word Allāh appears in the book, please add the glorification "*Subhāna-hu wa-Taʿālā*."
- Whenever the word Muhammad, or other words indicating Muhammad, e.g. Rasulullah, the Prophet, or Nabi appears, please add the prayer, "*Salla-llāhu ʿalaihi wa Sallam*." We have used (S) in the book to remind the prayer.
- Whenever the student comes across the names of a prophet or an angel, please add the prayer "*Alai-hi-s Salām*." This is noted by (A).
- For the first grade, this book does not introduce the Khalifas and the Sahabahs. However, the students should be taught to add the prayer "*Radi-allāhu ʿan-hu*" for a khalifa or a male companion of the Prophet (S). For a lady companion, the prayer "*Radi-allāhu ʿan-hā*" should be used.

Suggestions:

Please provide suggestions, corrections, ideas, etc., to improve the book by sending an e-mail to the publisher at weekendLearning@gmail.com. It is a combined effort of the publisher, authors, teachers and parents to prepare our future ummah. May Allāh guide us all! Amin.

Classwork
Weekend 1

Allah: *Our Creator*

Assalamu alaikum. Welcome to the class. Let us start by coloring this picture. Everything in this picture is made by Allah.

We pray to Allah. He made everything in this earth. Allah made all the people. He made all the animals, birds, and fishes. He made the dust and the big hills. Allah made the sun, the moon and all the stars. Allah made all of us. He is our **Creator**. He is all powerful. We pray to One and Only Allah.

Allah is not a man. Allah is not a woman. Allah has no shape. He does not have a body like us. We cannot see Allah but He can see us. Allah is not like us.

Allah is One. He does not have a daughter. He does not have a son. He does not have a father or a mother. He does not have a brother or a sister. He has no family. Allah is not like us.

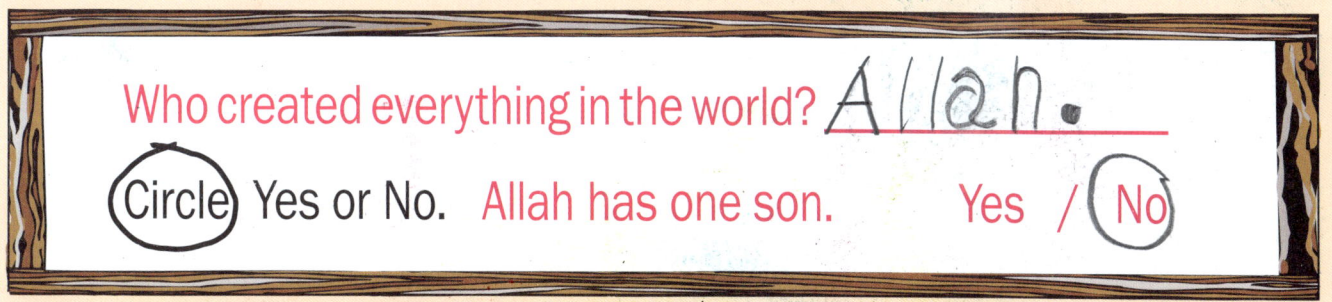

Who created everything in the world? _Allah._

Circle Yes or No.   Allah has one son.   Yes / **No**

Allah takes care of us every day and night. He gives us daylight to work. He gives us night to sleep. Allah gives us all the **seasons**. He gives us air to **breathe**. Allah gives us food and water. Allah gives us everything. We pray to One and Only Allah.

Allah has 99 beautiful names. We can pray to Allah using any of these names. **Ar-Rahman** and **Ar-Rahim** are two such names.

Allah gave us our family. He gave us our friends. Allah loves us so much that He sent us **prophets**. Prophets taught us how to be a good person. Muhammad (S) is the **Last Prophet** of Allah. Allah gave him a book called the **Qur'an**. The Qur'an teaches us how to lead a good life.

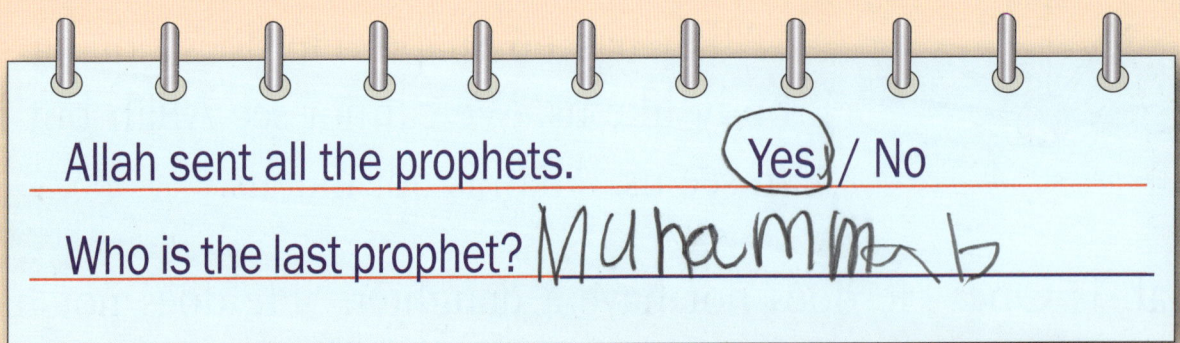

Allah sent all the prophets.   (Yes) / No

Who is the last prophet? Muhammad

Words that I learned today:

Creator • Seasons • Breathe • Ar-Rahman • Ar-Rahim • Prophets • Last Prophet • Qur'an

Homework Weekend 1

1. Write two things that Allah made.

   a. _____.

   b. _____.

2. ⓒircle the correct choice:

   a. Allah is a big and tall man.

   b. Allah has a body like us.

   c. Allah has no shape. He is not like us.

3. Fill in the blanks:

   We pray to One and Only _____.

   Allah is our C R __ __ __ __ R.

4. ⓒircle C for correct, W for wrong

Allah sent all the prophets.	C	W
Muhammad (S) is the FIRST prophet.	C	W
Qur'an is a Book from Allah.	C	W
Allah has 99 beautiful names.	C	W
Allah does not have any son or daughter.	C	W

5. Inside this box draw a picture of anything that Allah made for us.

Islam

Classwork
Weekend 2

Assalamu alaikum. Welcome to the class. Let us start by coloring this picture. This is the Kabah, a very special house in Makkah. Everyday, we pray to Allah by facing this house.

We are Muslims. We follow Islam. Islam is the **religion** given by Allah. A religion tells people how to live in this world.

Islam means **peace**. Islam teaches us to **obey** the rules of Allah. When we obey and listen to the rules of Allah, we get peace.

Islam is the only religion of Allah. We should not follow any other religion. Islam is a nice and easy religion. Islam teaches us how to be good people. If we follow Islam, our lives will be good.

What is the meaning of Islam? _____

Who gave us Islam? _____

Islam teaches us to believe in Allah. He is only one. We pray to Allah by doing **salat**. We cannot pray to anyone else.

Muslims live in every part of the world. They speak many languages. They look different. They wear different clothes. All Muslims read the Qur'an. The Qur'an is a book given by Allah. All Muslims obey Allah and follow Muhammad (S). He is known as **Rasulullah**.

Allah sent prophets to every part of the world. Prophets get message from Allah. All prophets taught us Islam. The first prophet of Islam is **Adam (A)**. The Last Prophet of Islam is Muhammad (S). Some other prophets of Islam are **Nuh, Ibrahim, Yusuf, Musa** and **Isa (A)**.

We follow Islam everyday.

What religion did all prophets teach? _____

Muslims obey Allah and Rasul.   Yes / No

Words that I learned today:

Religion • Peace • Obey • Salat • Rasulullah • Adam • Ibrahim • Yusuf • Musa • Isa

Homework Weekend 2

1. These words are jumbled up. Can you please organize them? (the first letter of the word is already placed for you.)

   L M S A **I**   I _ _ _ _ _

   A C E E **P**   P _ _ _ _ _

2. Circle **C** for correct, **W** for wrong

Islam is a game.	C	W
Allah gave us Islam.	C	W
The first prophet was Musa (A).	C	W
Muhammad (S) is known as Rasulullah.	C	W

3. Write the names of any three prophets of Islam:

   a. _____.

   b. _____.

   c. _____.

16

4. Circle the correct meaning of Islam:

   a. Peace.

   b. Prophet.

   c. Fight.

5. extra**credit**. Search the following words in the puzzle. The word **NUH** is already selected for you.

Our Faith

Classwork Weekend 3

Assalamu alaikum. Welcome to the class. Let us start by coloring this picture of a boy praying to Allah.

We are Muslim. We follow Islam. We **believe** in many things in Islam. If we believe then we have faith.

FAITH

1. We believe that there is only One Allah. We pray to Allah only.

2. We believe in the angels. Angels follow every order of Allah. Angels are made out of light. We are made out of clay.

3. We believe in the Books of Allah. Allah sent Books to many prophets. The Qur'an is the last Book of Allah.

4. We believe in all the prophets of Allah. In Arabic prophets are called **Rasuls**. Muhammad (S) is a Rasul of Allah. A rasul brings messages from Allah.

5. We believe that there will be a **Last Day**. On this day everything will end. Only Allah has no ending.

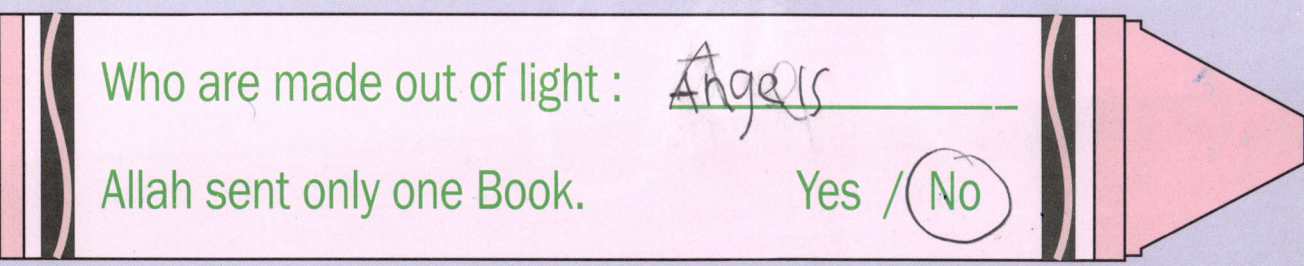

Who are made out of light : Angels

Allah sent only one Book.   Yes / (No)

6. We believe in the **Will of Allah**. This means nothing can happen without Allah's **permission**. If something good or

bad is going to happen to us, Allah knows that before it happens.

7. We believe that we will be raised after our death. Allah will be our **Judge**. If we do good things in this world, we will get **rewards**.

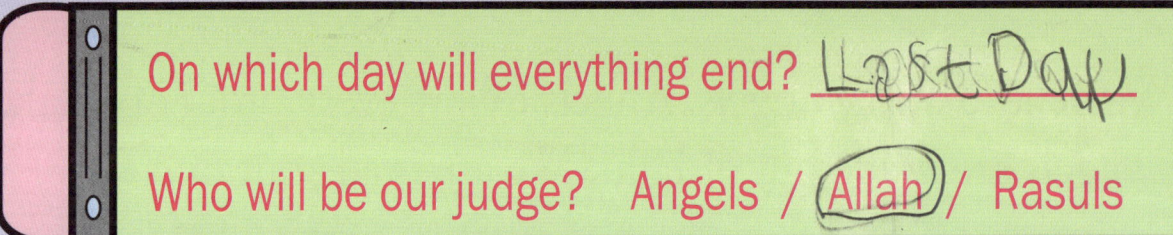

On which day will everything end? __Last Day__

Who will be our judge? Angels / (Allah) / Rasuls

Words that I learned today:
Believe • Rasuls • Messages • (Last Day) • Will of Allah • Permission • Judge • Rewards

Homework
Weekend 3

1. Put a (circle) around the correct answers:

   We pray to: angels / Qur'an / (Allah).

   Angels are made of: crayons / (light) / snow.

   Muhammad (S) was a: doctor / fisherman / (rasul).

   The Qur'an is the words of: my teacher / (Allah) / imam.

2. Fill in the blanks with the right word from the box:

Rasul	order	knows	raised
Judge		messages	

   Angels follow every __Order__ of Allah.

   A __Rasul__ brings messages from Allah.

   After death, we will be __raised__.

   Allah __knows__ everything.

   On the Last Day Allah will be our __Judge__.

   A rasul brings __messages__ from (Allah).

3. Circle **C** if it is correct, **W** if it wrong.

Allah sent only one book.	C	（W）
Allah knows if there will be rain next month.	（C）	W
A police officer will be our judge after we die.	C	（W）
Allah will reward us for our good work.	（C）	W

4. Write **Yes** if it is correct, and write **No** if it is wrong.

We believe that Allah has two brothers. _No_

On the Last Day, everything will end. _Yes_

We are made out of plastic. _No_

There are many angels. _Yes_

We believe in the Books of Allah. _Yes_

Prophet Muhammad (S)

Assalamu alaikum. Welcome to the class. Let us start by coloring this picture. This is the masjid of the Prophet (S). Let us color the dome green.

Muhammad (S) was born many years back in **Arabia**. His father's name was **Abdullah**. He died before Muhammad (S) was born. His mother's name was **Amina**. She died when Muhammad (S) was a young boy. Muhammad (S) grew up in a town called **Makkah**.

One day Muhammad (S) went to a cave to think. At night an angel came to him. He was Angel **Jibril**. He came with some words of the Qur'an. Muhammad (S) became a prophet of Allah.

Muhammad's (S) father of was: _Abdullah_

Who came to Muhammad (S) in a cave? _____

Prophet Muhammad (S) told everyone to be a good person. He told the people to **worship** one Allah. Some people of Makkah did not like him. They became very mean to the Prophet (S). Some of them wanted to kill him.

Our dear Prophet Muhammad (S) could not live in Makkah any more. He and other Muslims went to live in **Madinah**. Many people in Madinah became Muslims.

After many years, our Prophet Muhammad (S) came back to Makkah. People of Makkah then became Muslims.

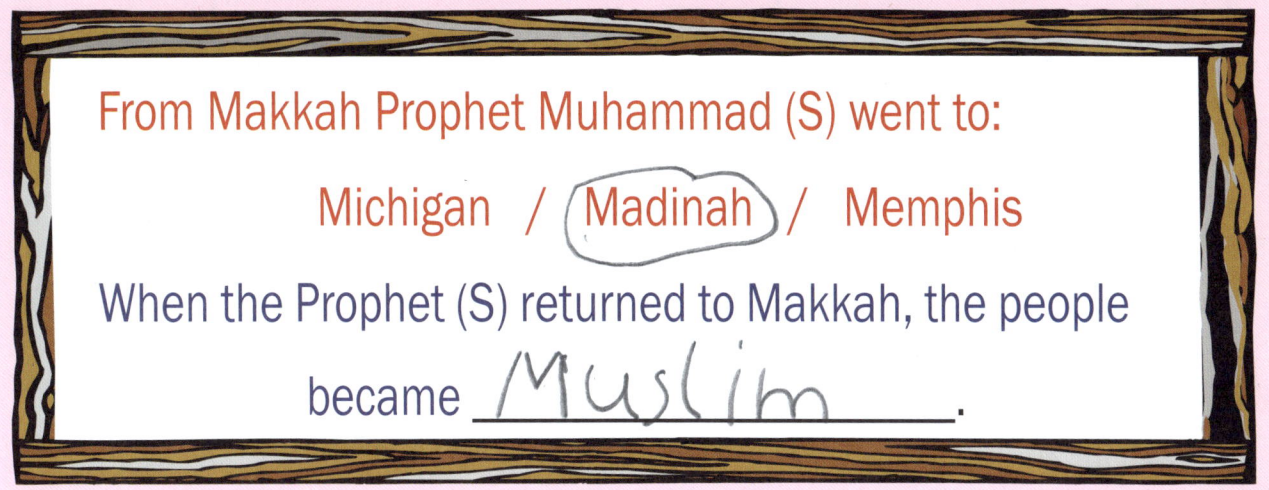

From Makkah Prophet Muhammad (S) went to:

Michigan / (Madinah) / Memphis

When the Prophet (S) returned to Makkah, the people became __Muslim__.

Prophet Muhammad (S) is the best person. He is the last prophet in Islam. We want to live the way Prophet Muhammad (S) had lived.

Words that I learned today:

Arabia • Abdullah • Amina • Makkah • Jibril • Worship • Madinah

Homework
Weekend 4

1. Circle **C** if the sentence is correct, **W** if it is wrong.

   Muhammad (S) is the First Prophet. ~~C~~ W

   Angel Jibril brought words of the Qur'an to Prophet Muhammad (S). C W

   People of Makkah made Muhammad (S) a prophet. C W

In questions 2 and 3 put a circle around the correct answer.

2. Prophet Muhammad (S) moved from Makkah to which town?
   (a) London.
   (b) Madinah.
   (c) New York.

3. Who was Prophet Muhammad's (S) mother?
   (a) Madinah.
   (b) Salima.
   (c) Amina.

4. Fill in the blanks.

   Prophet Muhammad (S) was born in ___Arabia___.

We should worship one __Allah__.

5. Match the words by drawing a line.

Qur'an — is an angel

Makkah — is a Prophet

Jibril — is a town

Muhammad (S) — is a Book

6. extra**credit.** Search the following words in the puzzle.

AMINA   ARABIA   JIBRIL   MADINAH
MAKKAH   PROPHET   WORSHIP   ALLAH

```
W O R S H I P R
U A M I N A H W
C R E H M P L H
S A L L A H M P
D B R T D U K G
J I B R I L J E
E A N B N W Q S
T F E T A Y C A
P R O P H E T U
```

The Qur'an

Assalamu alaikum. Welcome to the class. Let us start by coloring the word *Qur'an-ul Karim* in Arabic. Then color the Book.

The Qur'an is a Book of Allah. He sent the Book to Muhammad (S). The Qur'an is for all the people of the world. Allah sent the Qur'an in **Arabic**.

Arabic is a **language**. English is also a language. People of Arabia speak in Arabic. It is better to understand the Qur'an in Arabic. Sometimes people write the meaning of the Qur'an in other languages.

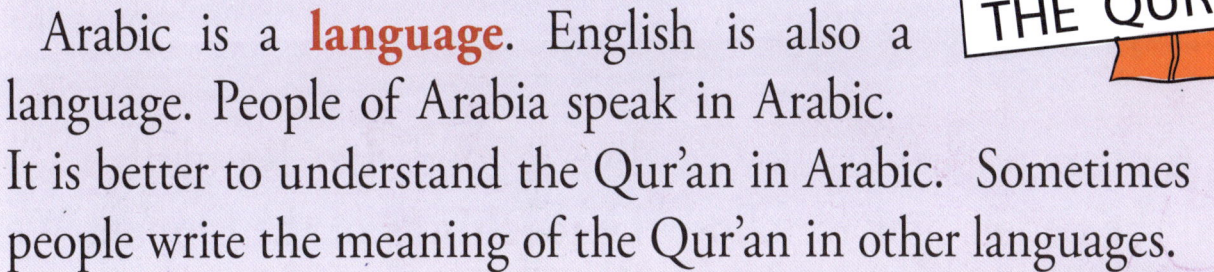

Who sent the Qur'an? _Allah_

What is the language of the Qur'an? _Arabic_

Angel Jibril **brought** the Qur'an to **Rasulullah (S)**. The whole book did not come in one day. Jibril brought it part by part. It took **23 years** to complete the Qur'an.

The Qur'an has **114 chapters**. The chapters are called **surah**. Some parts of the Qur'an came when Rasulullah (S) was in Makkah. Some other parts came when Rasulullah (S) was in Madinah.

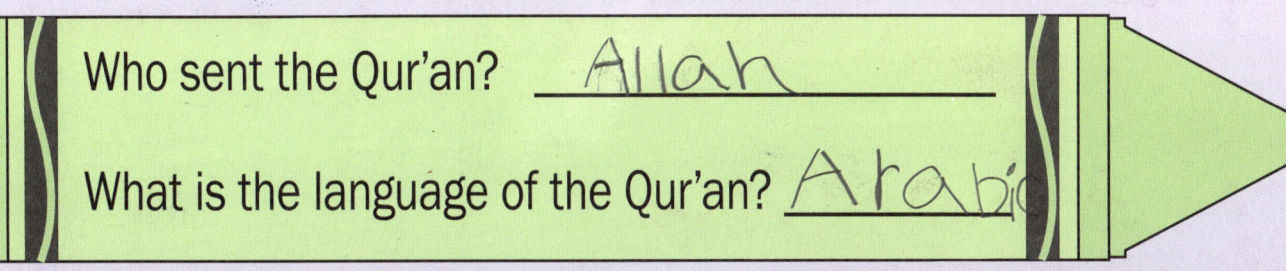

The Qur'an that we read today is the same as it came to Rasulullah (S). No word in the Qur'an has changed.

The Qur'an was sent in __23__ years.

The Qur'an has __114__ chapters.

The Qur'an teaches us how to live a good life. Rasulullah (S) showed the people how to follow the **teachings** of the Qur'an. We should read the Qur'an everyday.

Words that I learned today:
Arabic • Language • Brought • Rasulullah • Chapters • Surah • Teachings

Homework Weekend 5

1. Fill in the blanks

    The Qur'an has __114__ chapters.

    The language of the Qur'an is __Arabic__.

    Angel __Jibril__ brought the Qur'an to Rasulullah (S).

    The Qur'an was sent in two cities. These cities are known as __Madinah__ and __Makkah__.

2. Circle **C** if the sentence is correct, **W** if it is wrong.

    Allah sent the Qur'an in Chinese.   C **(W)**

    Words of the Qur'an are changed every year.   C **(W)**

    Muhammad (S) got the Qur'an in just 3 weeks.   C **(W)**

Put a circle around the correct choice in questions 3, 4 and 5.

3. Each chapter in the Qur'an is called:

    (a) Sunnah.

    (b) Surah.

    (c) Rasul.

4. The language of the Qur'an is:

(a) Arabic.
(b) French.
(c) German.

5. The Qur'an was completed in:

(a) 20 years.
(b) 23 years.
(c) 40 years.

6. **extracredit.** These letters are jumbled up. Can you please arrange them to make words? The first letter of the word is already given for you.

Q u r a n

J i b r i l

M A D I N A H

5 Pillars of Islam

Classwork
Weekend 6

Assalamu alaikum. Welcome to the class. Let us start by coloring the five pillars of a house.

Every house needs some **pillars**. Pillars hold up the roof. They support the house. Without pillars, a house will fall down.

If we think Islam to be our house, it has five pillars. These five pillars support the house of Islam. Without one of these pillars, the house will not stand up properly. Each of the pillars is important. If we do not make any of these pillars strong, we will be at loss.

1. The first pillar is **Shahadah**. It tells us that we believe in One Allah, and Muhammad (S) is His prophet. A person becomes Muslim by saying and believing in Shahadah.

2. The second pillar is **Salat**. These are the five daily prayers.

3. The third pillar is **Fasting**. During the month of Ramadan Muslims fast. They do not eat or drink during daytime.

4. The fourth pillar is **Zakat** or **charity**. We have to give part of our money to help the needy people.

5. The fifth pillar is **Hajj**. This is visiting Makkah at least once in our lifetime, if we can. Hajj is done in the 12th month of the Islamic calendar.

Islam has _____ pillars.

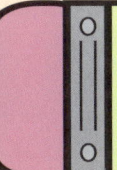

Which pillar stands for going to Makkah? _____

We should remember the five pillars and follow them. It will make us good Muslim. Our life will be happy and peaceful. Allah will give us His blessings.

In Ramadan Muslims: Fast.

Muslims give Zakat to needy people.

Words that I learned today:

Pillars • Shahadah • Salat • Fasting • Zakat • Charity • Hajj

Homework Weekend 6

1. How many pillars does Islam have? (Circle the right answer).

    (a) 3 pillars.
    (b) 4 pillars.
    (c) 5 pillars.

2. The meaning of Salat is: (Circle the right answer).

    (a) Going to Makkah.
    (b) Five daily prayers.
    (c) Giving money.

3. The meaning of Zakat is: (Circle the right answer).

    (a) A game.
    (b) Helping the needy.
    (c) Not eating or drinking.

4. The meaning of Fasting is: (Circle the right answer).

    (a) Running fast.
    (b) Not eating or drinking.
    (c) Eating quickly.

5. If the pillars of a house break down, what will happen to the house? (Circle the right answer).

(a) The grass will not grow.

(b) The house will fall down.

(c) The house will become a school.

6. Fill in the blanks with the right word from the box:

| Makkah   Five   One   Prophet |

We believe in ___One___ Allah.

Muhammad (S) is a ___prophet___ of Allah.

Hajj is done in ___Makkah___.

We pray ___Five___ times everyday.

Shahadah: *The First Pillar*

Assalamu alaikum. Welcome to the class. Let us color this sentence and the raised finger. It reminds us that there is only One Allah.

Last week, we learned about the five pillars of Islam. We now know that the first pillar is **Shahadah**. In Arabic, we say:

لَا إِلَهَ إِلَّا اللهُ مُحَمَّدٌ رَسُولُ اللهِ

La ilaha illal-lahu Muhammadur Rasulullah.

This means: "There is no one to worship except Allah; and Muhammad is His Rasul or Prophet."

The first part of Shahadah is: There is no one to worship except Allah. It means that we should not worship anyone other than Allah. It means that we should not worship any **idols**, pictures, people, sun or moon. We should pray to Allah only. As Muslims, we must say Shahadah, and believe that only Allah is our God.

The second part of the Shahadah tells us to believe that: Muhammad (S) is the Rasul of Allah.

We believe that Prophet Muhammad (S) received the Qur'an from Allah. He taught us the **messages** of Allah. We do not worship Prophet Muhammad (S). He is Allah's **Rasul**. We love him and **respect** him. We want to live the way Rasulullah (S) lived.

Words that I learned today:
Shahadah • Idols • Messages • Rasul • Respect

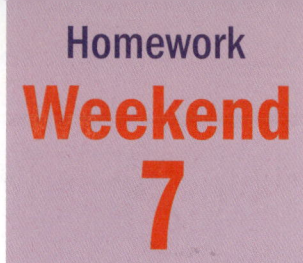

Homework
Weekend 7

1. Let us color the Arabic text of the Shahadah with coloring pencils.

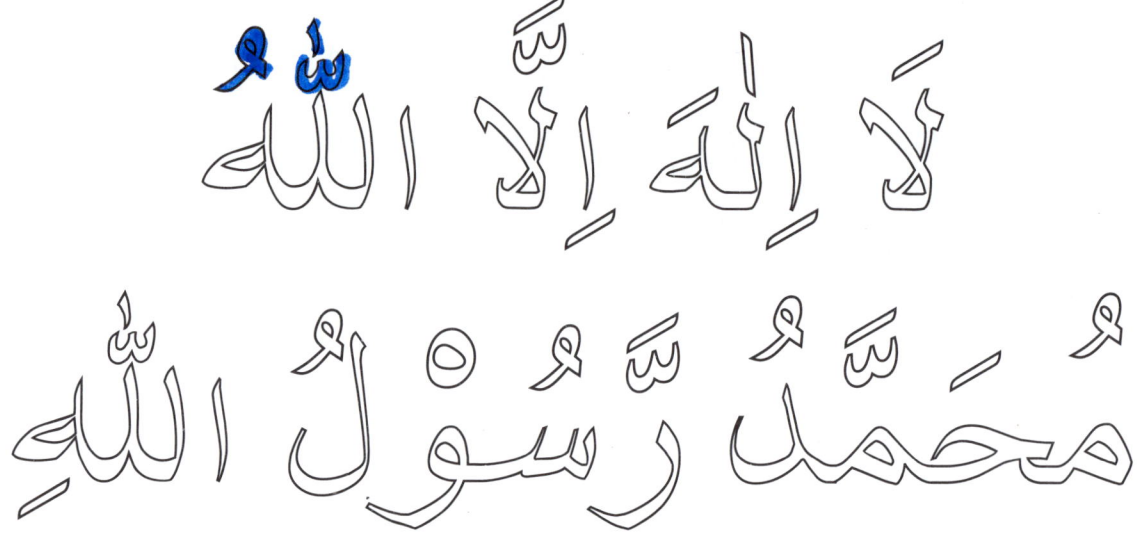

2. Memorize the Shahadah with the help of your parents.

3. Let us read the story, then in the next page circle C for correct acts and W for wrong acts.

Sarah is a 6 year old girl. She wants to pray to Allah. She loves Allah very much. One day she wanted to draw a picture of Allah. She thought for a while and then gave up. Because she did not know how Allah looks like. Nobody knows how Allah looks like. Then her mom told her, "we do not worship a picture.' Sarah will never draw a picture to worship.

Sarah wants to pray to Allah. C W

Sarah loves Allah very much. C W

Sarah wanted to draw a picture of Allah. C W

Mom said we should not worship a picture. C W

Sarah will never worship a picture. C W

4. extra**credit.** Search the following words in the puzzle.

Salah: *The Second Pillar*

Classwork
Weekend 8

Assalamu alaikum. Welcome to the class. Let us start by coloring this picture of a rug on which we can make salah.

The second pillar of Islam is **Salah**. Salah is our daily prayer. We make salah **five times a day**. These five salah are called:

1. Fajr   - Very early in the morning, before sunrise
2. Dhuhr   - Soon after noon
3. Asr   - In the afternoon
4. Maghrib - After sunset
5. Isha   - At night

When we make salah, we face the direction of a house called **Kabah** in Makkah.

For salah, we should have clean body and clean clothes. To clean our body, we make **wudu** before salah. We wash our hands, face, head and feet. We make salah on a clean place.

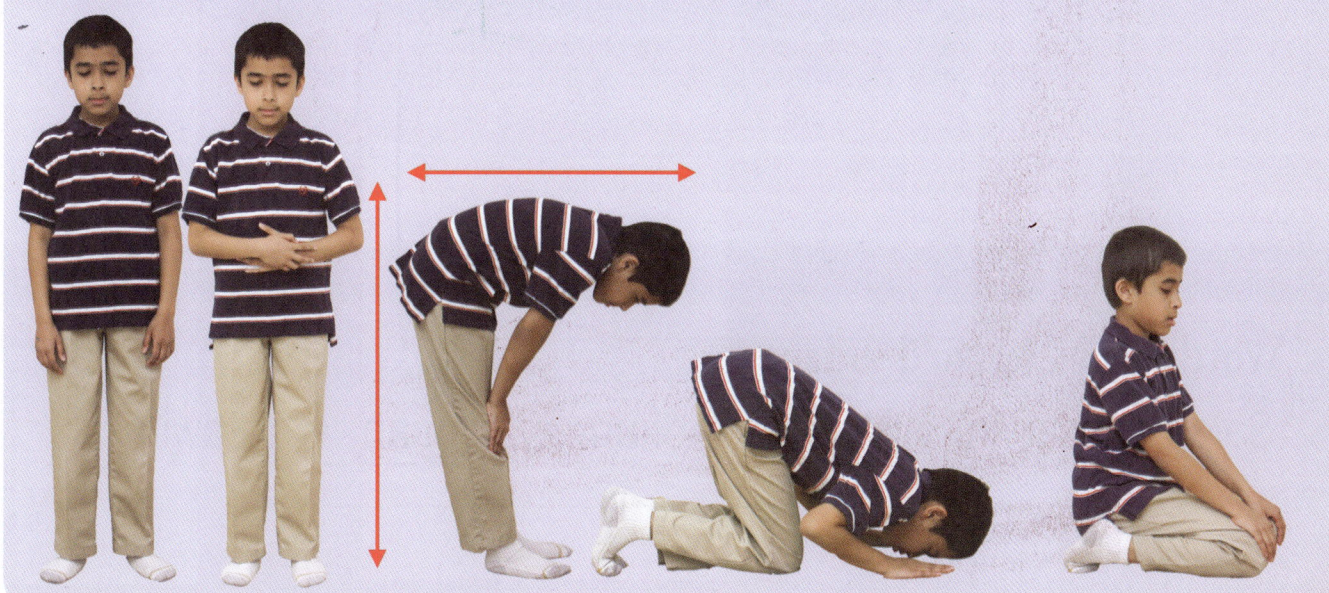

The call for salah is **Adhan**. When you hear Adhan, come to salah quickly. You can make salah alone. It is better to make salah with others.

> What '*house*' do we face for salah? _KABAH_
>
> Cleaning the body for salah is called _WUDU_
>
> The call for salah is known as _ADAH_

There are many other types of salah. On Fridays, we make a special salah in the masjid with many people. This salah is called **Jumuah**. In the month of Ramadan people do a special salah called **Tarawih**.

If we do not make salah everyday, Allah will not be happy with us. Children and grown-ups in the family should do salah. Allah tells us to make salah on time. Salah gives us peace and success.

Words that I learned today:

Salah • Kabah • Wudu • Adhan • Jumuah • Tarawih

Homework
Weekend 8

1. Arrange the salat as these are done in a day.

   Dhuhr   2

   Isha   5

   Fajr   1st

   Maghrib   4

   Asr   3

2. Which direction do we face for salat? (Circle the right answer).

   (a) Any house.
   (b) A masjid in New York.
   (c) The Kabah.

3. When do we make wudu? (Circle the right answer).

   (a) After going to bed.
   (b) Before salat.
   (c) After salat.

4. When is adhan called? (Circle the right answer).

   (a) Before salat.
   (b) In the middle of salat.
   (c) After salah.

5. When adhan is called, we should: (Circle the right answer).

   (a) Go out to play.
   (b) Go to bed quickly.
   (c) Come for salat.

6. Circle **C** if it is correct, **W** if wrong.

   We should do salat on time.   C   W

   We can skip salat all week but make it up on Sundays.   C   W

   Only grown-ups need to make salat, children and old people need not do it.   C   W

   Kabah is in Makkah.   C   W

   Makkah is in Texas.   C   W

Fasting: *The Third Pillar*

Classwork
Weekend 9

Assalamu alaikum. Welcome to the class. Imran is excited to see the Ramadan moon. Can you please color the picture?

47

Fasting is the third pillar of Islam.

In each year there is a special month called **Ramadan**. This is a month in Arabic **calendar**. Like other Arabic months, it starts when we see a **thin moon**. The month ends when we see another thin moon.

In Ramadan Muslims fast every day. **Fasting** means not eating or drinking during daytime. We break the fast after the sun sets. We cook many good foods for the evening meal. This meal is called **Iftar**. It is good to share your Iftar with others. You can take the food to the masjid, or invite other families to your home.

We break our fast with a meal called:	*Iftar*
In which month do Muslims fast?	*Ramadan*

Fasting teaches us to give up bad things and be good people. Fasting brings us closer to Allah. Allah rewards us when we fast. During Ramadan we pray to Allah much more. People pray a special salat called **Tarawih**.

Little children like you may try to fast for a few hours. Next year, you may try to fast for a few more hours. When you are older, you will be able to fast everyday of Ramadan like other grown-ups.

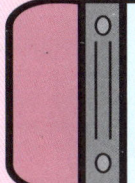 The special prayer in Ramadan is: _Tarwih_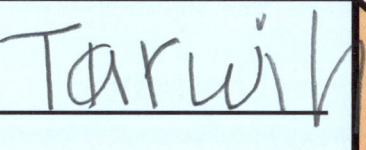

Ramadan is a great month. Many years back Allah started sending down the Qur'an in the month of Ramadan.

When Ramadan ends, we have **Eid**. We do not fast on the day of Eid. It is a day of joy and happiness. We share our happiness with friends, relatives and also with others who do not have enough.

Words that I learned today:
Ramadan • Calendar • Fasting • Iftar • Tarawih • Eid

Homework
Weekend 9

1. Fill in the blanks using the right words from the box.

   Daytime   Eid   Ramadan   Iftar

   What is the month for fasting? _Ramadan_

   What is the meal for breaking fast? _Iftar_

   What is the special day after Ramadan? _Eid_

   While fasting, we cannot eat during: _Daytime_

2. On the day of Eid we: (Circle the right answer).

   (a) Share our food with friends and family.
   (b) Do not see friends.
   (c) Fast for the entire day.

3. In Ramadan, during daytime grown-up Muslims: (Circle the right answer).

   (a) Drink milk.
   (b) Drink water.
   (c) Do not eat anything.

50

4. Ramadan is for: (Circle the right answer).

   (a) One week.

   (b) One month.

   (c) 10 days.

5. Circle **C** for correct, **W** for wrong.

   Ramadan starts with Eid.   C   **W**

   Allah started to send the Qur'an in the   C   W
   month of Ramadan.

   Ramadan ends when we see a full moon.   **C**   W

Zakat: *The Fourth Pillar*

Classwork
Weekend 10

Assalamu alaikum. Welcome to the class. Let us start by coloring this picture where two children are helping a needy man.

Zakat is the fourth pillar of Islam. The word Zakat means to make you pure. It also means giving something to the poor. It is a type of **charity**. Charity is when we give something to help someone else. Let us understand why Zakat is so important in Islam.

Every day we wear good clothes. We eat good food. We live in good homes. These good things are **blessings** of Allah.

It is sad that not everyone in the world gets a full meal everyday. Many kids sleep hungry every night. Many families do not have a home. Some people do not have a job. Many people are **needy**. Allah tells us to help the needy people. We should share our blessings with others.

4th pillar of Islam is called:	_Zakat_
Zakat is a type of:	Flower / Angel / **Charity**
Allah wants us to help the	_needy_ people.

We can help the needy people with Zakat. Usually people give money as Zakat. Some people give food or clothes as Zakat.

Rich people cannot get Zakat money. We give Zakat to the needy people. With Zakat money they can **solve** their problems. Our money can help needy families to build a home, start a business or buy food or medicine. They can do things so that they will not remain poor. In a few years they may have enough money to give zakat to other needy people.

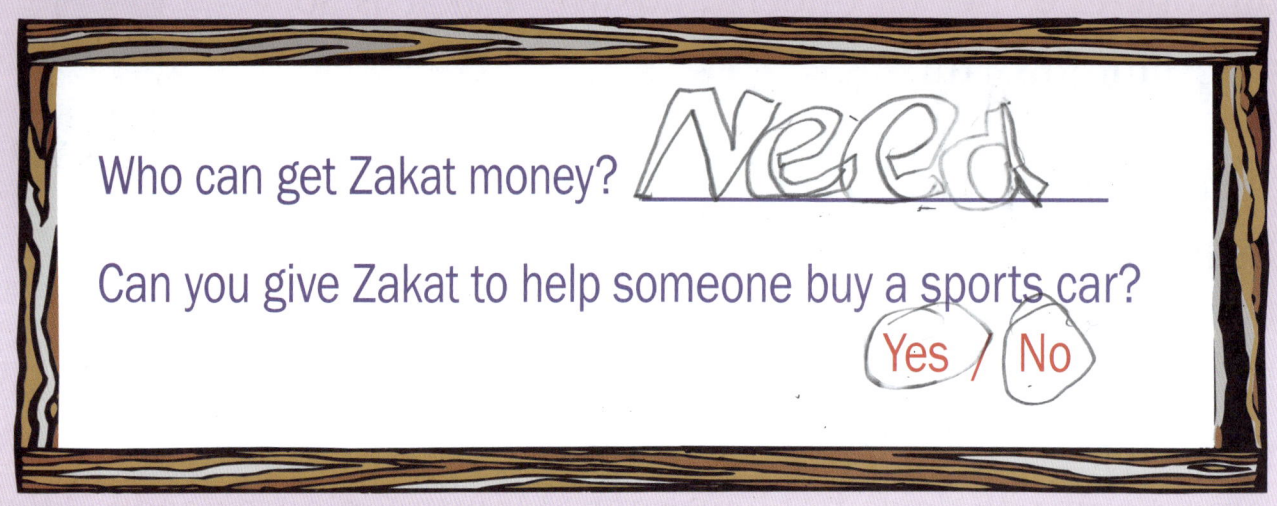

Who can get Zakat money? _Need_

Can you give Zakat to help someone buy a sports car?

Yes / **No**

We can give Zakat at any time of the year. We give zakat on our income and savings. Many people give Zakat in the month of Ramadan. They calculate their annual income and find out how much to give in Zakat. If a person does not have enough money, he need not pay Zakat.

Words that I learned today:

Zakat • Charity • Blessings • Needy • Solve

Homework
Weekend 10

1. We can help others more if we do not waste. Cross out the plate that shows waste after finishing lunch.

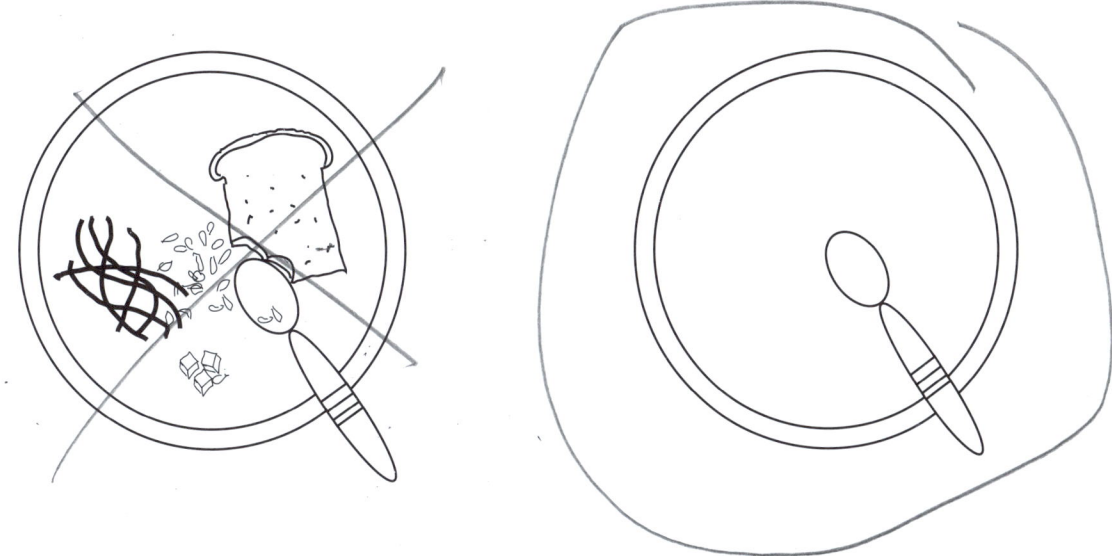

2. Below is a list of some items. A poor person is asking you to give him zakat money to buy some items from the list. Cross out the items for which you may NOT give him zakat money.

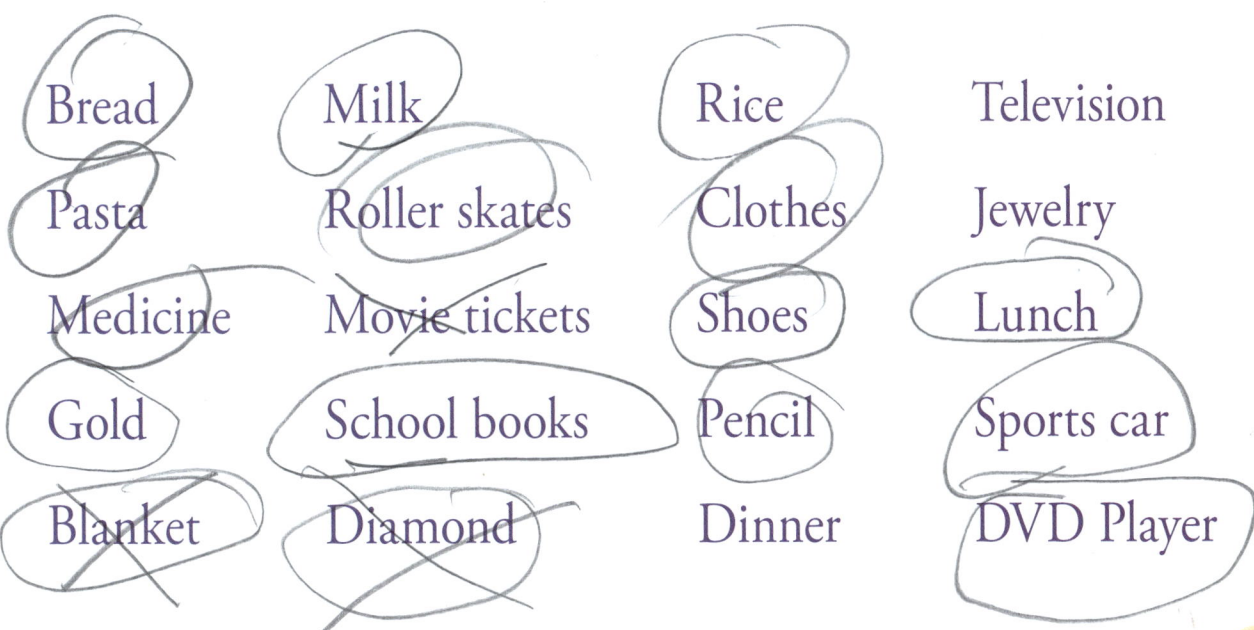

3. **extracredit.** Circle **Yes** if correct, circle **No** if wrong.

A family lost their home in a flood. They have no food. Can we give them zakat? — ~~Yes~~ No

A boy wants a game for his PlayStation. Can we give him zakat? — Yes ~~No~~

We can give zakat to the rich people. — Yes   No

Zakat money helps the needy people. — Yes   No

Hajj: *The Fifth Pillar*

Classwork Weekend 11

Assalamu alaikum. Welcome to the class. Can you trace the path to the Kabah?

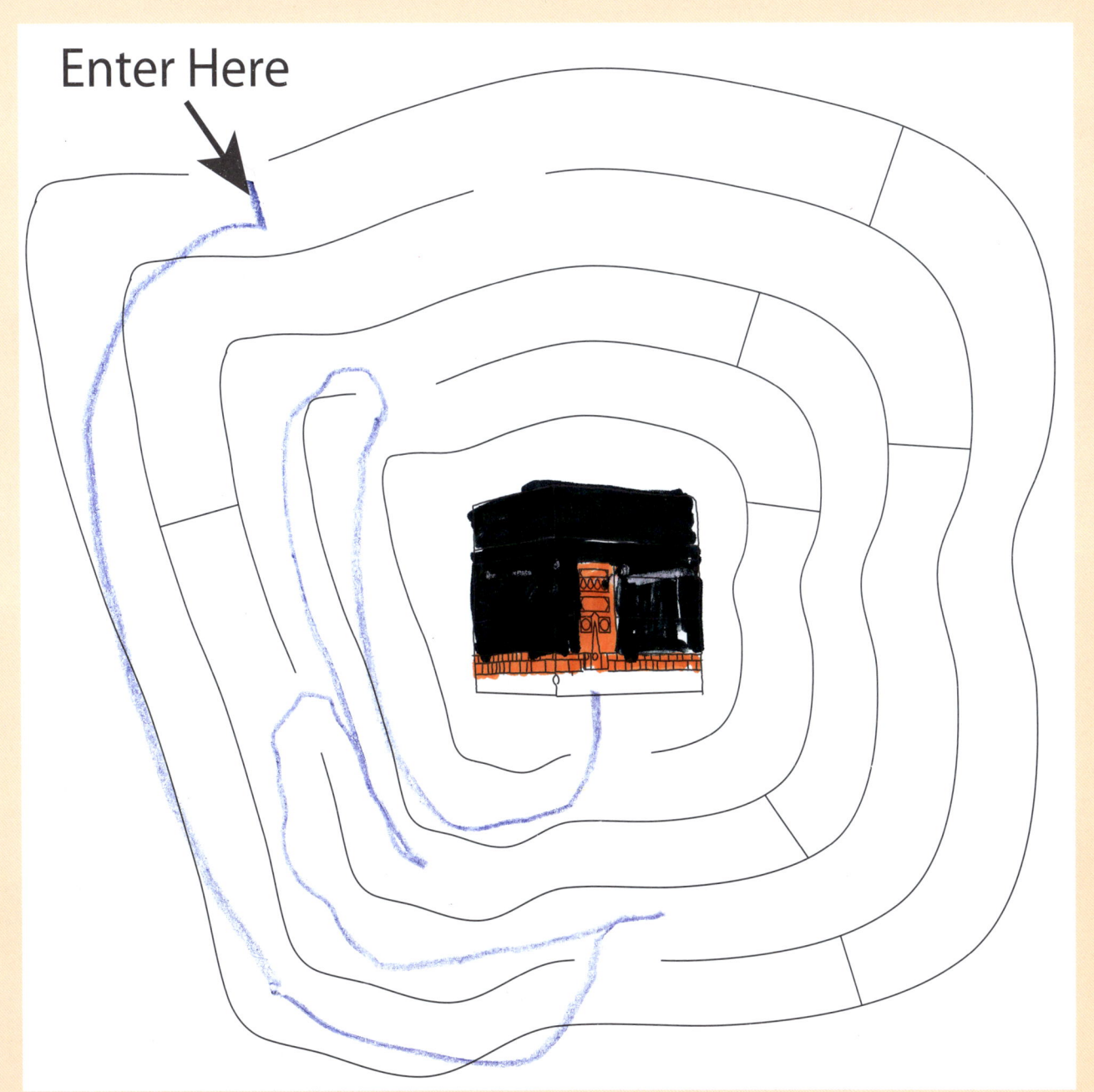

Islam has 5 pillars. **Hajj** is one of the pillars of Islam. During Hajj, we go to Makkah. If we can, we should do Hajj at least once in our life.

During Hajj, we remember the teachings of Prophet **Ibrahim (A)**. We learn to avoid the **Shaitan**. We also learn to **sacrifice** for the sake of Allah. We learn that Allah helps the good people when they are in difficulty. Hajj teaches us to be kind, patient and **humble**. A humble person is not proud.

During Hajj we remember prophet ___Islam___

Where do people go to do Hajj? ___Nik___

Hajj is held once every year in Makkah. Hajj is done in the 12th month of the Islamic calendar. During Hajj, men wear two pieces of white clothes, called **Ihram**. All men look similar in the same type of white clothes. Men and women walk around the Kabah. The Kabah is a black house in Makkah inside a large masjid. Nobody lives in the house.

People do many other duties during Hajj. All the people also stay in tents. People spend their time in praying to Allah.

Hajj is a call from Allah. Several **million** Muslims from all over the world answer this call every year and come for Hajj.

58

When Hajj ends we have **Eid-al Adha**. It is a **festival** for the Muslims. Even if we are not in Hajj, we sacrifice an animal on that day. We share the meat with family, friends and the needy.

During Hajj men wear a cloth called: _____

The festival at the end of Hajj is: _____

Words that I learned today:
Hajj • Ibrahim • Shaitan • Sacrifice • Humble • Ihram • Million • Eid-al Adha • Festival

Homework Weekend 11

1. Circle **C** for correct, **W** for Wrong.

   Hajj is a teaching of Ibrahim (A).   C W *(C circled)*

   Hajj is held several times a year.   C W *(W circled)*

   During Hajj men wear colorful clothes.   C W *(W circled)*

   Hajj can be done in Canada.   C W *(W circled)*

   Hajj is not a pillar of Islam.   C W

2. Fill in the blanks using the right words from the box

   | ~~Humble~~ ~~Makkah~~ ~~Million~~ ~~Hajj~~ ~~Eid~~ |

   Several __Million__ Muslims come to Hajj.

   Hajj teaches us to be kind and __Humbr__.

   Hajj is done in __Makkah__.

   __Hajj__ is a call from Allah.

   After Hajj there is an __Eid__.

3. Circle the correct choice.

   A family came back from Hajj. Where did they come from?

   (a) London.
   (b) Tokyo.
   (c) Makkah.

4. **extracredit.** Circle the correct choice.

   If Eid-al Adha is today, Hajj is:

   (a) Already done.
   (b) Next week.
   (c) Next month.

   If a man is wearing Ihram, maybe he is:

   (a) Doing Hajj.
   (b) Going to work.
   (c) Playing soccer.

Saying Bismillah: *Remembering Allah*

Classwork
Weekend 12

Assalamu alaikum. Welcome to the class. Let us start by coloring this picture of Jameel. He says Bismillah before reading any book.

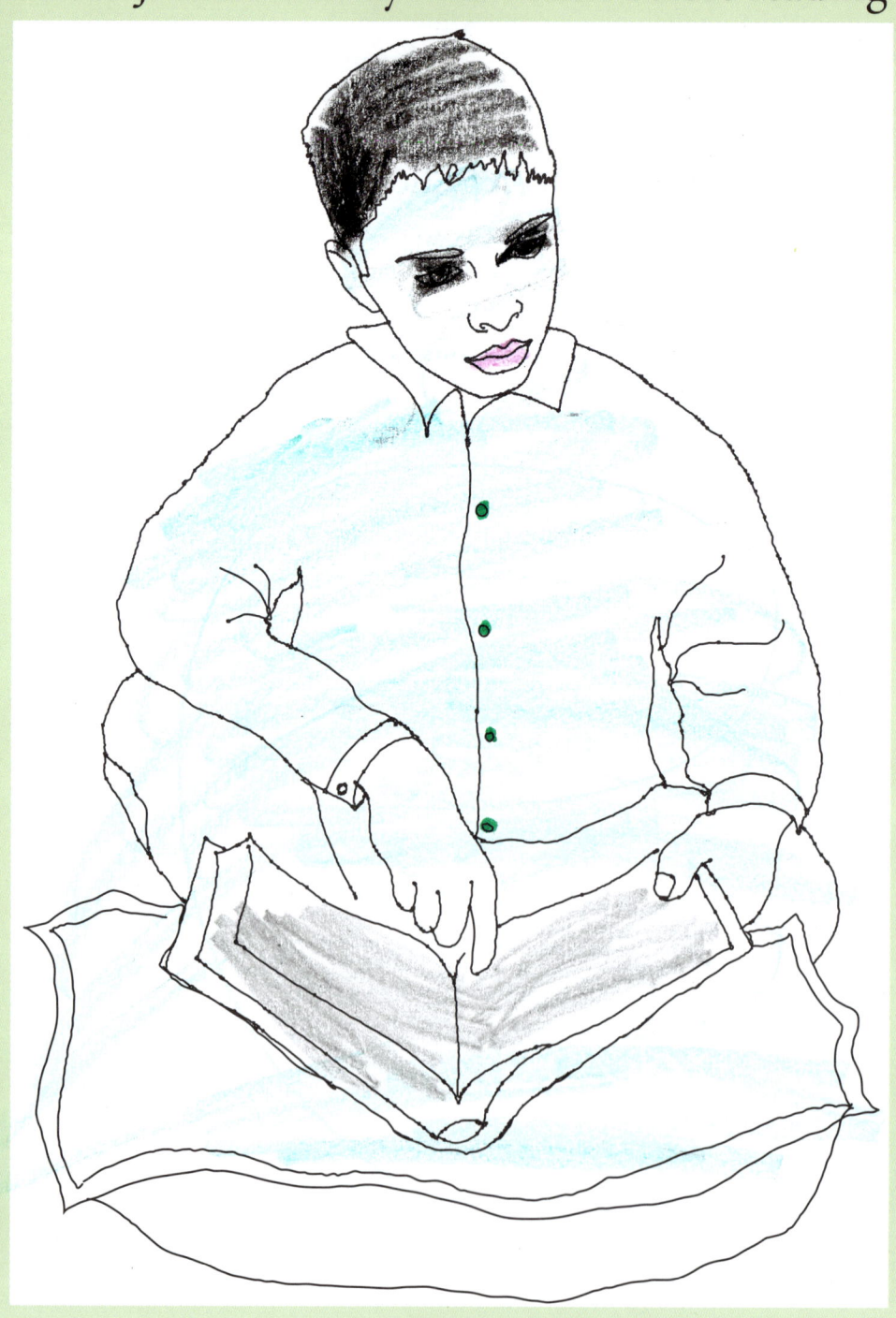

Everyday, we do many things. We pray, read, eat, talk and play. We cannot do anything if Allah does not want us to do.

We should remember Allah when we do any work. We remember Allah by saying "**Bismillah**." We should say Bismillah before we do anything.

Bismillahir Rahmanir Rahim means "In the name of Allah, most Kind, most Rewarding.

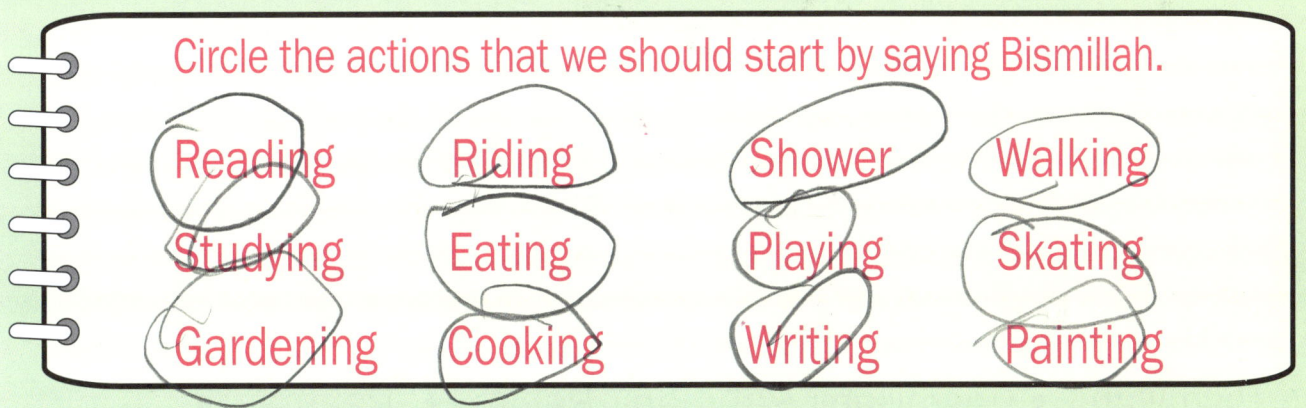

Circle the actions that we should start by saying Bismillah.

Reading   Riding   Shower   Walking
Studying Eating   Playing   Skating
Gardening Cooking   Writing   Painting

Allah is **Rahman**, or Kind, because He gives us so many things even if we do nothing. He gave us the sun and the moon, and we did not do anything for these. He made fresh air for us even before we were born. He made different seasons for us. He gave us eyes, ears, and nose. We did not do anything to get these.

Allah is **Rahim** because He **rewards** us whenever we do something good. He rewards us when we pray. He rewards us with knowledge when we study. He rewards us with money when we work. He rewards us with happiness when we are nice to others.

We always remember Allah by saying "Bismillahir Rahmanir Rahim." When we eat, we say Bismillah. This reminds us that the food is a gift from Allah. We say Bismillah when we start to read the Qur'an. The Qur'an is a gift from Allah. When we get into the car, we say Bismillah. When we play, we say Bismillah. We say Bismillah before we do anything.

Words that I learned today:
Bismillah • Bismillahir Rahmanir Rahim • Rahman • Rahim • Reward

Homework Weekend 12

1. Circle the actions that we should start with Bismillah.

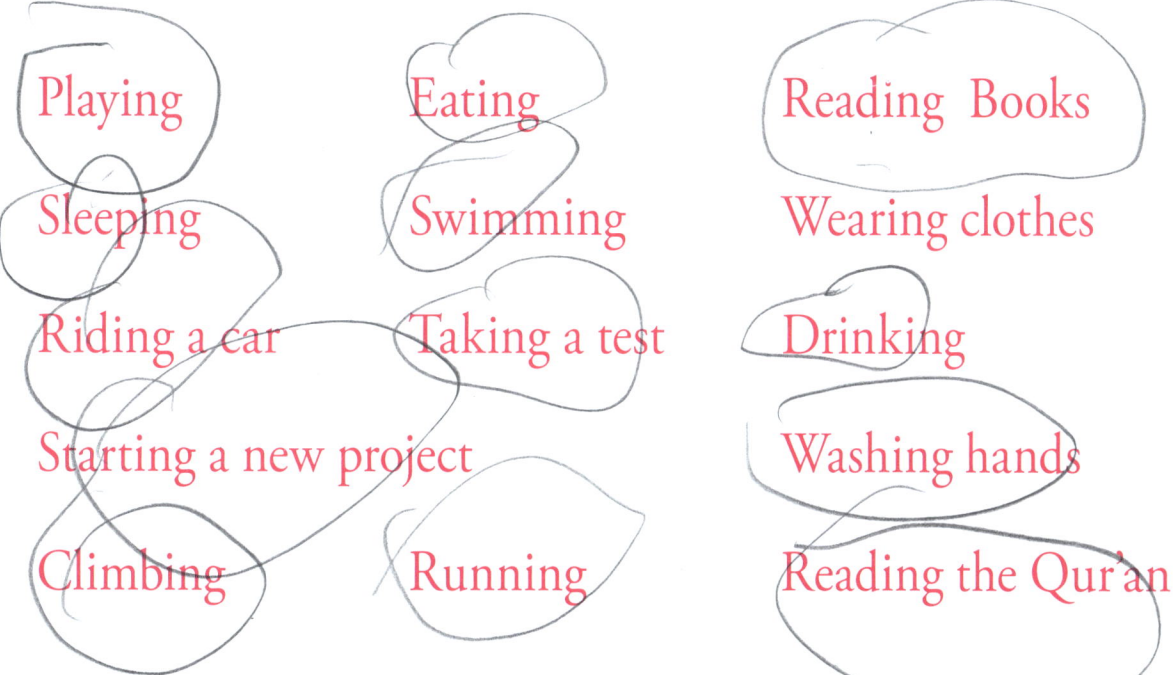

Playing	Eating	Reading Books
Sleeping	Swimming	Wearing clothes
Riding a car	Taking a test	Drinking
Starting a new project		Washing hands
Climbing	Running	Reading the Qur'an

2. Saying Bismillah reminds us of Allah's gifts to us. Circle the things that are gifts from Allah.

Lake	Grass	Trees	Family	Hand
Skin	Earth	Summer	Eyes	Flower
Apples	Milk	Books	Rain	Winter
Day	Nose	Brother	Ear	Rocks
Water	Sister	House	Clothes	Fingers

3. Write **Yes** if correct, **No** if Wrong.

Allah helps us to eat. _Yes_

Allah helps us to read. _Yes_

Allah helps us to play. _Yes_

Allah helps us to sleep. _Yes_

Allah helps us to be happy. _Yes_

Allah gives us peace. _Yes_

Allah helps us learn. _Yes_

Angels: *They Always Work for Allah*

Classwork
Weekend 13

Assalamu alaikum. Welcome to the class. Let us start by coloring this picture. In this mountain is the Cave Hira, where Angel Jibril brought messages of Allah to Muhammad (S).

Allah created **angels**. They are created out of light. We cannot see them. As Muslims we should believe in angels. They are not scary, they are good beings.

Angels are all around us. They help us. They watch us and protect us. Angels write down any good work that we do. They also write down any bad thing that we do.

There are many angels. They do many types of jobs. Jibril is the name of one angel. He came to Prophet Muhammad (S). Angel Jibril used to bring **ayat** of Qur'an to the Prophet (S).

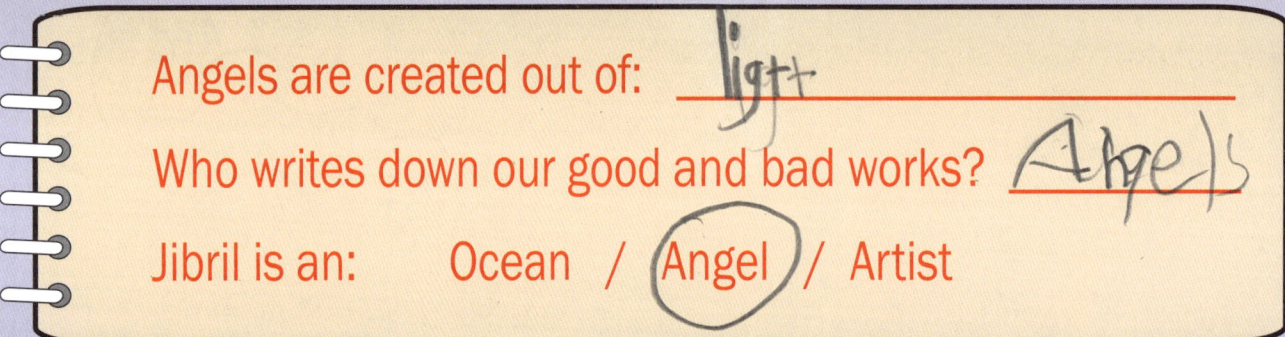

Angels are created out of: ___light___

Who writes down our good and bad works? ___Angels___

Jibril is an: Ocean / (Angel) / Artist

Angels always praise Allah. They work for Allah. They never say no to Allah.

After Allah created human beings, all the angels showed respect to them. This is because human beings are better than the angels.

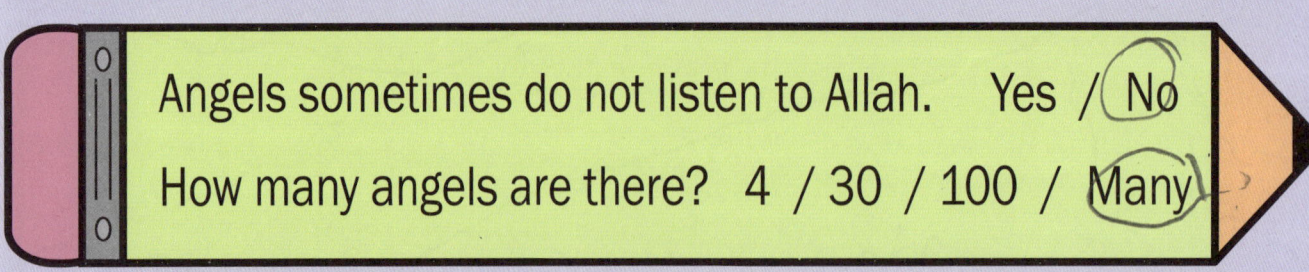

Angels sometimes do not listen to Allah. Yes / (No)

How many angels are there? 4 / 30 / 100 / (Many)

Once Rasulullah (S) was in a **battle**. The enemies were strong. They had many **soldiers**. Muslims had only a few soldiers. Because Muslims were good people, Allah helped them by sending many angels. The enemies lost the battle.

After doing a hard job for a long time, sometimes it becomes easy. Do you know how it became easy? Allah helped you by sending angels. They help us in our good work.

Words that I learned today:
Angels • Ayat • Battle • Soldiers

Homework
Weekend 13

1. Circle the right choice.

   Angels are made of:

   (a) Wood.
   ((b)) Light.
   (c) Gold.

   Angels help people in their:

   (a) Bad work.
   ((b)) Good work.

   When Allah asks the angels to do something, they:

   ((a)) Do it quickly.
   (b) Go to sleep.
   (c) Forget.

2. Mark ✓ if it is correct, and mark ✗ if it is wrong.

   Angels helped the enemies of the Prophet (S).

   Some angels work for bad people.

Angels protect us.

Angel Jibril brought the Qur'an to the Prophet (S).

3. Fill in the blanks with the right word from the box

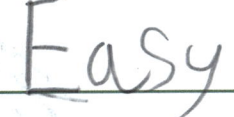
Cave Hira ✓   Light ✓   Write ✓   Easy ✓

Angels can make our hard job __Easy__.

Angel Jibril came to the Prophet (S) in __Cave Hira__.

Angels are made out of __Light__.

Angels __Write__ our good and bad works.

4. These letters are jumbled up. Can you please arrange them to good words?

 __Battle__

 __Light__

  __Cave Hira__

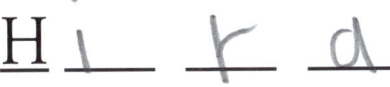

Classwork
Weekend 14

Shaitan: *Our Enemy*

Assalamu alaikum. Welcome to the class. Let us start by coloring this traffic sign. We will not walk on Shaitan's path.

We learned that angels help us in our good work. When Allah created human being, angles showed them respect. But **Shaitan** did not show them respect. He became our enemy.

Allah made everything in the **Universe**. He made us from **clay**. He made angels out of light, and made Shaitan out of fire. We cannot see Shaitan.

Shaitan was created out of: ____friend____

Shaitan is our friend.   Yes / (No)

Allah made Shaitan to **test** us. When we pass the test, we become better people.

Shaitan is not a scary **monster** as in your comic books. He does not talk in a scary voice. He talks in our mind in a nice way, but he tells us to do bad things. He tells that you will have fun if you do bad things. When it is Fajr time, he tells you to keep sleeping as the bed is so warm. He will make you forget the salah.

Shaitan **whispers** in our mind. He tells us that he is our best friend. But he is not our friend. If we believe him, he will make us do bad things or tell lies. Sometimes, he will make our friends tell us to do bad things.

 How does Shaitan speak in our mind? _Whise_

We should be very careful about Shaitan. If we do a bad thing, it is Shaitan's plan. If we have a bad idea, it is from Shaitan. We should never listen to him. We should never follow his orders.

Words that I learned today:
Shaitan • Universe • Clay • Test • Monster • Whisper

Homework
Weekend 14

1. Mark ✓ if it is correct, and mark ✗ if it is wrong.

   Shaitan tells us to listen to the teacher. ✗

   Shaitan tells us to shout in the class. ✓

   Shaitan tells us to read the Qur'an. ✗

   Shaitan tells us to hurt others. ✓

   Shaitan tells us to miss our salat. ✓

2. Write **S** if told by Shaitan, write **A** if told by angels.

   Make salah on time. — A

   Play during salah. — S

   Help your parents. — A

   Break the toys and the dishes. — S

   Fast in Ramadan. — A

   Keep yourself clean. — A

3. Trace the road that you want to take.

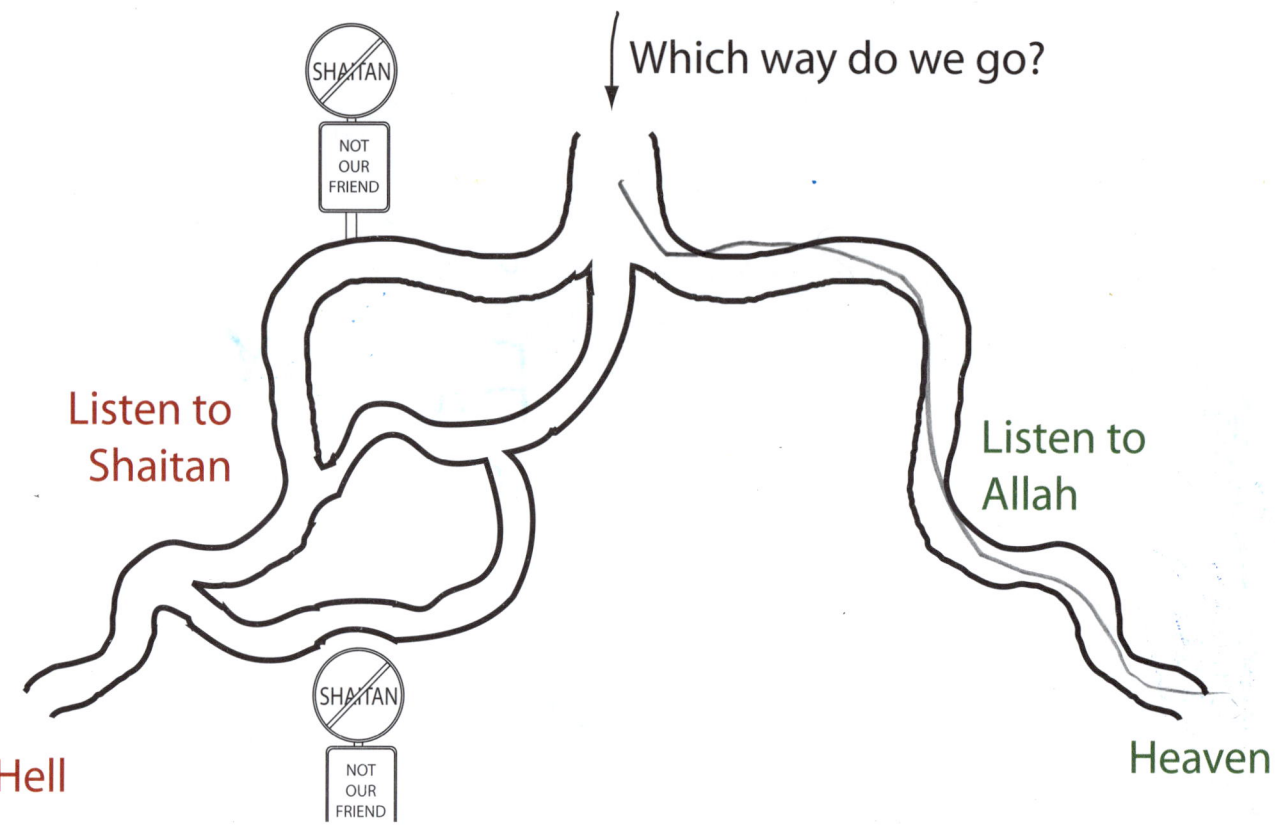

Adam (A): *The First Prophet*

Assalamu alaikum. Welcome to the class. Let us start by coloring this picture. Before Adam (A), there were no people on this earth.

A long time back, thousands of years ago, Allah decided to place people on the earth. He made Adam (A) out of **clay**.

Adam (A) was the first prophet. Allah taught him many things. Adam (A) was **intelligent**. Allah gave him **knowledge**. He learned names of everything. The angels saw that Adam (A) knew many things. So they agreed to show him respect.

Adam (A) was created out of: _____

What did Adam (A) learn from Allah? _____

Iblis, who was Shaitan, did not want to show respect to the people. He was very **proud** because he was made out of fire. He thought he was better than the people. Shaitan said he will make people do bad things.

Adam and his wife lived happily in the Garden. Allah told them not to listen to Shaitan. One day Shaitan came to them with bad ideas. He told them lies. Adam forgot about what Allah told them. He and his wife listened to Shaitan. Then they became sorry for listening to Shaitan. Adam and his wife prayed to Allah to **guide** them. Allah forgave them and guided them.

Adam (A) and his wife had many children. The children and their families went all over the world. We all are children of Adam (A). All the people of the world are from a big family.

From the story of Adam (A) we learned that we should never listen to Shaitan. We should always follow Allah's teachings.

Iblis was made out of _____

Shaitan gave good ideas to Adam.   Yes / No

Words that I learned today:

Clay • Adam • Intelligent • Knowledge • Iblis • Proud • Guide

Homework
Weekend 15

1. Adam (A) was made out of: (Circle the right answer).

    (a) Clay.

    (b) Bricks.

    (c) Iron.

2. Iblis is a: (Circle the right answer).

    (a) Firefighter.

    (b) Shaitan.

    (c) Bird.

3. Angels agreed to help the: (Circle the right answer).

    (a) People.

    (b) Shaitan.

    (c) Fish.

4. Allah gave Adam (A): (Circle the right answer).

    (a) A book.

    (b) Knowledge.

    (c) A car.

5. Search the following words in the puzzle.

IBLIS   ADAM   GARDEN   CLAY   NAMES

extra**credit**: PROUD (search backwards!)

```
H  I  B  L  I  S
G  A  R  D  E  N
I  D  U  O  R  P
N  A  M  E  S  K
R  M  C  L  A  Y
```

6. Take the words from this box and fill in the blanks:

| proud   angels   garden   guide |

Adam (A) and his wife lived in the _____.

Iblis was _____ as he was made of fire.

Adam (A) asked Allah to _____ him.

The _____ saw that Adam (A) knew many things.

81

Nuh (A): *Saved From The Great Flood*

Classwork
Weekend 16

Assalamu alaikum. Welcome to the class. Let us start by coloring some of the animals that may have been in the Boat of Nuh (A).

Long ago there was a land where many bad people lived. They would lie, steal, and hurt other people. They also worshipped idols and false gods. To guide them, Allah sent a prophet. His name was **Nuh (A)**.

Nuh (A) told the people to listen to Allah. He told them to be good. He told them there is no god but Allah. Nuh (A) tried his best. Many people made fun of him. They would not listen to him. So, Allah decided to **punish** the bad people. Allah would bring a big **flood**.

Allah told Nuh (A) to build a big boat. Nuh (A) collected a lot of wooden **planks** in an open dry field. He started to tie them up with ropes. The bad people would walk by him and laugh at him. "What a silly person!" They thought. "He is building this big boat in the dry field. We never get any water here!"

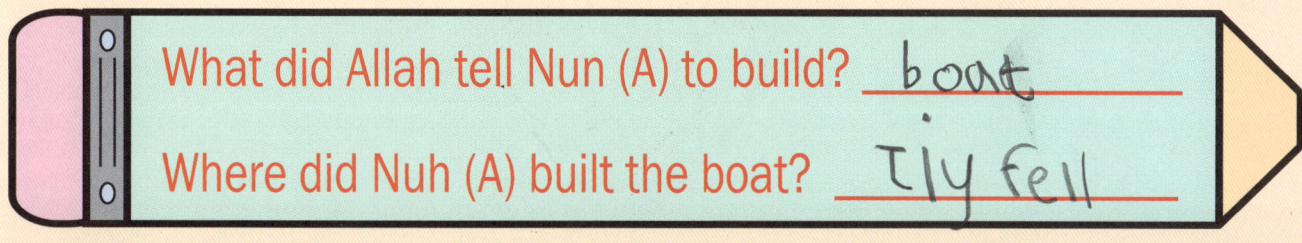

What did Allah tell Nun (A) to build? __boat__

Where did Nuh (A) built the boat? __Tiy fell__

One day Nuh (A) finished building the boat. Allah told Nuh (A) to get all the good people and **a pair of each kind of animal** on the boat. A pair of chicken, a pair of duck, a pair of lamb, and goats, and cows and so on.

Then one day it started to rain. And it rained even more. Even harder. It rained for many days. The ponds filled up. The lakes filled up. The rivers filled up. Then there was a flood. The boat that Nuh (A) built started to float. The **waves** became bigger and higher. The good people were safe on the boat. All the bad people died under the water.

A few days later the sun came out. The boat landed on a dry place when the flood ended. Nuh (A) and the good people got off the boat. They set up a new **village**. Now, everyone in the village was good people.

On the boat Nuh (A) took a pair of _____

Allah punished the bad people with a _____

Words that I learned today:

Nuh • Punish • Flood • Planks • Pair • Wave • Village

Homework
Weekend 16

1. Fill in the blanks with the right word from the box.

> good ✓   prophet ✓   flood ✓

Too much rain can make a __flood__.

Allah helps __good__ people.

Nuh (A) was a __prophet__.

2. Allah told Nuh to build a: (Circle the right answer).
   - (a) Boat. ⭕
   - (b) Car.
   - (c) House.

3. When it rained, the boat: (Circle the right answer).
   - (a) Sank.
   - (b) Floated. ⭕
   - (c) Flew.

4. Nuh (A) took a pair of: (Circle the right answer).
   - (a) Books.
   - (b) Toys.
   - (c) Animals. ⭕

5. All the people in the boat were: (Circle the right answer).

   (a) Good.

   (b) Bad.

   (c) Angry.

6. Circle **C** if it is correct, **W** if it is wrong.

   The boat of Nuh (A) was made of steel. C W

   After the flood ended, there were many bad people. C W

   Allah saves good people. C W

7. Search the following words in the puzzle.

   NUH   FLOOD   PAIR   WAVE
   PLANKS   BOAT   RAIN

W	E	R	B	T	G	T
A	F	L	O	O	D	A
V	P	L	A	N	K	S
E	A	U	T	U	V	C
N	I	S	K	H	E	S
F	R	A	I	N	L	O

Ibrahim (A): *Never Listen to Shaitan*

Assalamu alaikum. Welcome to the class. Let us start by coloring this picture of a Jamarah, a place where Ibrahim (A) chased away the Shaitan. When people go for Hajj, they throw small rocks at this wall.

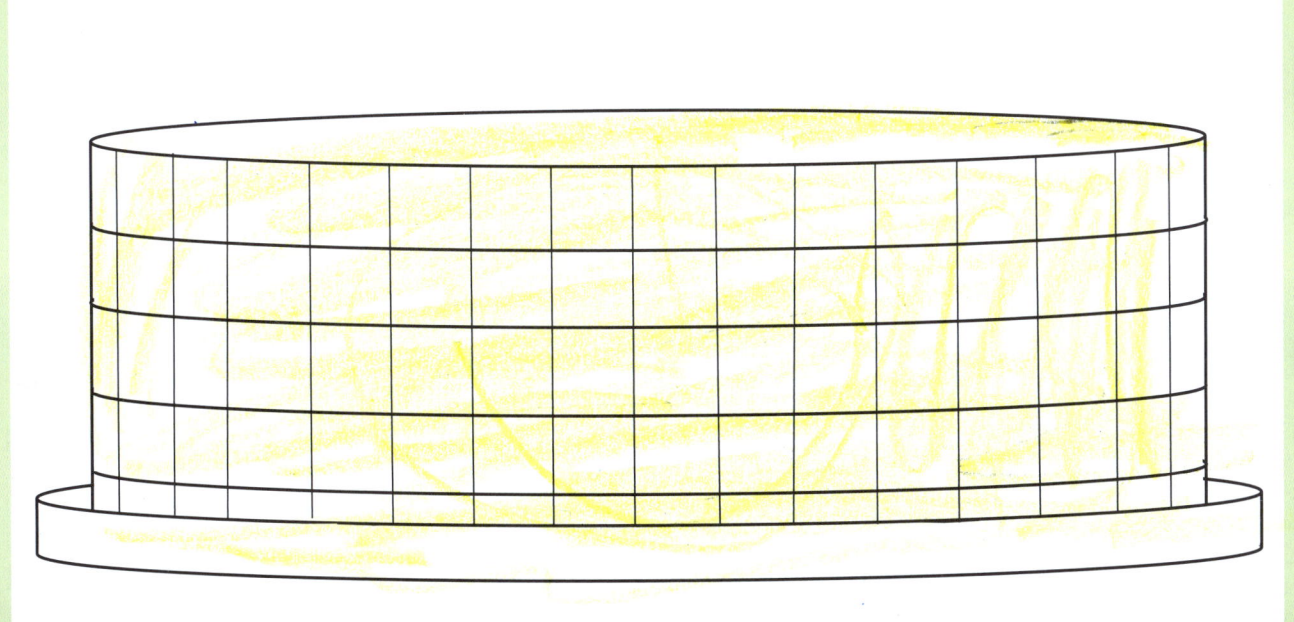

Long ago many people in a town worshipped **idols**. They used to make and sell idols. They did not worship Allah. To guide these people Allah sent a prophet. His name was **Ibrahim (A)**.

Ibrahim (A) loved his family very much. He told his families and relatives to worship one Allah. His father still wanted to worship idols. Many other people also worshipped idols. They would not listen to Ibrahim (A). Ibrahim (A) loved his family so much that he prayed to Allah for them.

Who in Ibrahim's (A) house worshipped idols?

his father

Ibrahim (A) had two sons, **Ismail (A)** and **Ishaq (A)**. One day Ibrahim (A) brought his baby son Ismail (A) and his mother **Hajar** to a **lonely** desert. Allah wanted the baby and his mother to live in the desert. Ibrahim (A) was sure that they will be safe with Allah. Surely, Allah saved them. Allah gave them spring water in the desert. This is **Zamzam** water. Later, this desert area became the town of Makkah. Many people started to live in Makkah.

In Makkah both Ibrahim (A) and Ismail (A) built the **Kabah**. We make our Salat facing the Kabah. Ibrahim (A) started the **Hajj**

in Makkah. Muslims go to Makkah to do Hajj. When we go to Hajj, we remember Ibrahim (A) and his family.

Ibrahim (A) loved his children very much. He taught them to make regular Salat. Ibrahim (A) always prayed to Allah for them. They never listened to bad ideas from Shaitan. When Ismail (A) and Ishaq (A) grew up, they too became prophets.

The spring in Makkah is called _Zamzam_

Who was the mother of Ismail (A)? _Hajar_

Words that I learned today:

Idols • Ibrahim • Ismail • Ishaq • Hajar • Lonely • Zamzam • Kabah • Hajj

Homework Weekend 17

1. Circle **T** for true and **F** for false.

   Ibrahim (A) had two bad sons. ~~T~~ F

   Ibrahim (A) told people not to worship idols. T ~~F~~

   Ismail (A) and Nuh (A) built the Kabah. T ~~F~~

   We make our salat to Jamarat. T ~~F~~

2. Fill in the blanks with the words from this box.

   | Kabah ✓ Ibrahim (A) Zamzam ✓ |

   Allah gave spring water to Mother Hajar and Ismail (A). This spring is called the _Zamzam_.

   Ibrahim (A) and Ismail (A) built the _Kabah_.

   Prophet _Ibrhim (A)_ told others not to worship idols.

3. Ibrahim (A) brought baby Ismail (A) and Mother Hajar to:

   (a) A lonely desert. ← circled

   (b) A city.

   (c) A forest.

4. Ibrahim (A) told people to worship:

   (a) Idols.

   (b) Prophets.

   (c) One Allah.

5. Kabah is located in:

   (a) Madinah.

   (b) Makkah.

   (c) Jamarah.

6. These letters are jumbled up. Can you please arrange them to make good words?

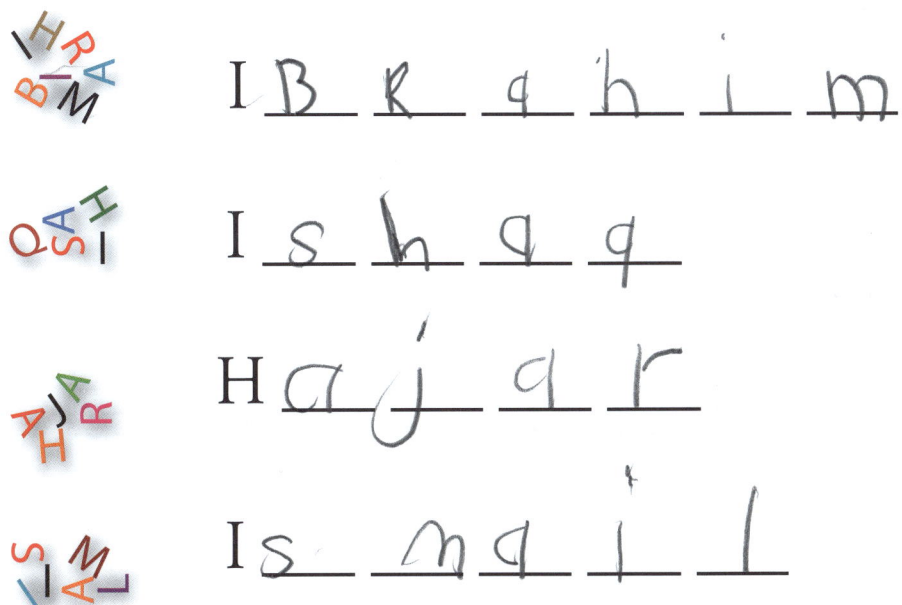

Musa (A): *A Good Man Against a Bad Ruler*

Classwork
Weekend 18

Assalamu alaikum. Today we will color this picture of pyramids. The rulers of Egypt built the pyramids.

Once upon a time, there was a bad **ruler** in a country called **Egypt**. People were very sad with this ruler. The ruler made the poor people work very hard. They worked day and night to make beautiful palaces for the ruler. The ruler forced them to make big **pyramids**.

One day, the ruler learned that a little boy from the poor people will create problem for him. "Kill all the little boys," ordered the bad ruler.

One of the poor families had a little boy named Musa. His mother was worried. "Would the king kill my little Musa?" she thought. She knew Allah could save anyone. She put baby Musa (A) in a **basket** and placed the basket in the river. The basket floated and reached the **palace** of the ruler. The queen saw the lovely baby and wanted to raise him. She also wanted to hire a woman to look after the baby. Do you know whom the queen hired? It was Musa's mother!

Such was the beautiful plan of Allah. The ruler wanted to kill all little boys. But Musa (A) grew up in his mother's care in the same ruler's palace! The ruler could not kill Musa (A).

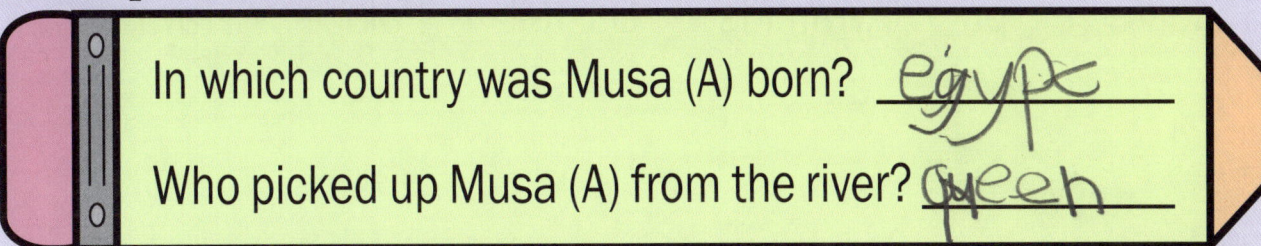

In which country was Musa (A) born? _egypt_

Who picked up Musa (A) from the river? _queen_

When Musa (A) grew up, he became a prophet. Allah gave him a book called **Tawrat**. He told the ruler about Allah. He showed the ruler some proofs that there is Allah. The ruler did not believe because he thought he was god. Finally Allah destroyed the ruler and his people.

Musa (A) helped the poor people in Egypt. He freed them from the bad ruler's country.

Musa (A) received a book named: _Tawrat_

Allah loved the ruler in Egypt.   Yes / **No**

Allah helped the poor people in Egypt.   **Yes** / No

Words that I learned today:

Ruler • Egypt • Pyramids • Basket • Palace • Tawrat

Homework
Weekend 18

1. Musa (A) was born in: (Circle the correct choice.)

    (a) China.
    (b) India.
    (c) Egypt. ⭕

2. The basket carrying Musa (A) reached the: (Circle the correct choice.)

    (a) Pyramids.
    (b) Ruler's palace. ⭕
    (c) Mountain.

3. The bad ruler wanted to kill the: (Circle the correct choice.)

    (a) Birds.
    (b) Boys. ⭕
    (c) Fishes.

4. Write your answers in the given spaces.

    In the ruler's palace, who took care of Musa (A)?

     mother

    Where did Musa's (A) mother put the basket?

     riLer

5. We learn many things from the life of Musa (A).

   Mark ✓ if it is correct, and mark ✗ if it is wrong.

   We should make the poor people work hard. ✗

   Allah can save anyone. ✓

   It is good to help the poor people. ✓

   The rulers who built the pyramids were very kind. ✗

   Musa (A) showed the ruler some proof of Allah. ✓

6. Search the following words in the puzzle.

   EGYPT ✓ PYRAMID ✓ MUSA ✓ QUEEN ✓ FREE ✓

   extra**credit**.   BASKET   PALACE (Search upside down!)

   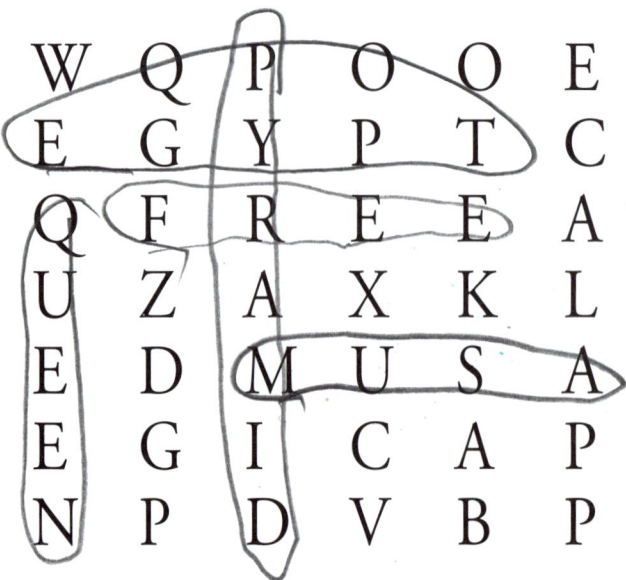

Isa (A): *A Good Son of a Good Mother*

Classwork Weekend 19

Assalamu alaikum. Welcome to the class. Let us start by coloring this book. Allah gave Isa (A) a Book called Injil.

Hundreds of years after Musa (A), Allah sent another prophet. His name was **Isa (A)**. In English we know him by the name **Jesus**. He came to guide the people of Musa (A).

Isa's (A) mother was **Maryam**. She was an honest woman. She followed the teachings of Allah. She was a good Muslimah. Allah **blessed** her with a good son, Isa. When Isa (A) grew up, Allah made him a prophet. Some people thought mother Maryam and her son Isa were evil.

Some people think that Isa (A) was a son of Allah. We know that Allah does not have a son or a daughter. Allah does not have a father or a mother.

Like other prophets, Isa (A) too told his people to be good. He told his people to do salat and pay zakat. Some of his own people did not like him. They gave him very hard time. They wanted to kill Isa (A). But they could not kill him.

What is the name of Isa (A) in English? _____

Who was the mother of Isa (A)? _____

Allah gave a Book to Isa (A). This Book is called **Injil**. The Book that Allah sent to Muhammad (S) is the Qur'an. Isa (A) taught that there is only one Allah. Believing in one Allah is called **Tawhid**. He told his people to worship none but Allah.

Isa (A) was poor. His true followers were poor too. Even with all the difficulties in life, he never gave up faith in Allah.

From the life of Isa (A), we learn that we should follow the teachings of Allah. It is important to be good. Even if people are bad with us, we should always be good and follow the path of Allah.

Allah gave Isa (A) a book called: _____

Isa (A) told his people to worship: _____

Words that I learned today:
Isa • Jesus • Maryam • Blessed • Injil • Tawhid

99

Homework
Weekend 19

1. Mark ✓ if it is correct, mark ✗ if it is wrong.

    Prophet Musa (A) came after Isa (A). ☐

    Isa (A) and Maryam were brother and sister. ☐

    Allah does not have any children. ☐

    Prophet Isa (A) was a good Muslim man. ☐

    Maryam was an honest woman. ☐

Circle the right choice in question 2, 3, 4 and 5.

2. The book that Allah gave to Isa (A) is called:
    (a) Qur'an.
    (b) Injil.
    (c) Bedtime Stories.

3. Tawhid is to believe in:
    (a) One Allah.
    (b) Injil.
    (c) Musa (A).

4. We should always try to be on the path of:

    (a) Allah.

    (b) The play ground.

    (c) The bad people.

5. All the prophets told their people to:

    (a) Play.

    (b) Be good.

    (c) Be a prophet.

6. Draw lines connecting the sentence to the right words.

The Book of Muhammad (S) is	Musa (A)
The Book of Isa (A) is	Tawhid
Believing in One Allah is	Qur'an
Isa (A) came to guide the people of	Injil

Makkah and Madinah

Classwork
Weekend 20

Assalamu alaikum. Welcome to the class. Let us color this map of Arabia. Color the sea blue, and the land brown.

Two places in Arabia are very important. One is the city of Makkah and the other is Madinah. Makkah is a big city. In this city is the Kabah, which is our **Qiblah**. It is the direction of our Salat. When we stand up for Salat, we face towards the direction of Kabah. Near the Kabah is a fountain of water called **Zamzam**. Both the Kabah and the Zamzam are inside a very large masjid, called **Al-Haram**.

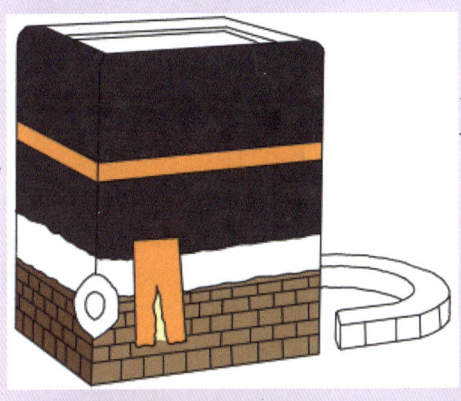

Every year, millions of Muslims from every part of the world come to Makkah for Hajj. Muslims also come to Makkah for **Umrah**. It is a smaller type of Hajj. Umrah can be done at any time, but Hajj should be done only in the month of Hajj.

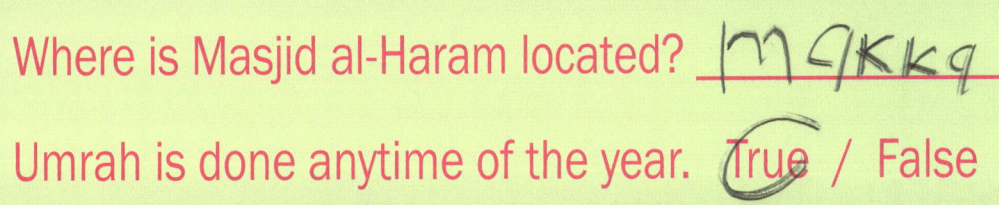

Where is Masjid al-Haram located? _Makka_

Umrah is done anytime of the year. **True** / False

Our dear Rasulullah (S) was born in Makkah. He received a part of the Qur'an when he lived in Makkah.

Rasulullah (S) received the other part of the Qur'an in another city named **Madinah**. This city is about 200 miles north of Makkah. Sometimes this city is called **Madinatun-Nabi** or City of the Prophet. This city has many green trees.

Madinah has several important **masajid**. One of them is the Prophet's Masjid. This masjid is very large and beautiful. Rasulullah (S) made the first masjid in a place called **Quba** in Madinah. There is another masjid in Madinah that has **two Qiblah**! Only one Qiblah is now used for Salat.

Where can you find the Prophet's (S) Masjid? _Madinah_

Madinah is **South** / **West** / **East** / **North** of Makkah.

Words that I learned today:
Qiblah • Zamzam • Al-Haram • Umrah • Madinatun-Nabi • Masajid • Quba

Homework Weekend 20

1. Makkah and Madinah are in: (Circle the right answer)

    (a) Japan.
    (b) **Arabia.** ⭕
    (c) Egypt.

2. Qiblah is the direction of our: (Circle the right answer)

    (a) ~~Salat.~~ ⭕
    (b) **Umrah.** ⭕
    (c) School.

3. The large Masjid in Makkah is: (Circle the right answer)

    (a) Zamzam.
    (b) Al-Haram.
    (c) **Quba.** ⭕

4. Fill in the blanks.

    Where do people go for Hajj? _Makkah_

    Where do people go for Umrah? _Makkah_

    Where is a masjid with two Qiblah? _Madinah_

5. Circle **C** if it is correct, **W** if it is wrong.

The Kabah is inside Masjid Al-Haram.	**C**	W
Rasulullah (S) was born in Madinah.	C	**W**
Zamzam is our Qiblah.	C	**W**
Madinah has Prophet's Masjid.	C	W

6. extra**credit**.

Find a map of the world. On the map, find Arabia. If it is a big map, try to find Makkah and Madinah.

Then mark ✓ if you found the place, mark ✗ if you could not find the place.

Arabia ☐   Makkah ☐   Madinah ☐

Good Manners

Assalamu alaikum. Welcome to the class. Tawfeeq raises his hand before he talks in the class. This is a good manner. Can you please color Tawfeeq?

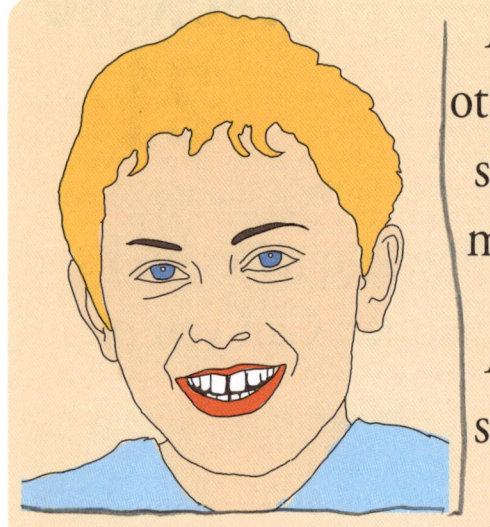

Allah loves those who **behave** nicely with others. When we are nice to others, we show good manners. We can practice good manners everywhere.

At home or in the classroom, we should talk softly. We show respect to everyone—old or young. When we meet someone, we say "Assalamu Alaikum." This **greeting** means "may peace be on you." If someone greets us saying Assalamu Alaikum, we reply by saying "Wa Alaikum Salam."

When we have guests, we greet them nicely. We should have good manners while eating. We should not talk with food in our mouth. We should not waste food. When we go to someone's home, we should be very careful about their things.

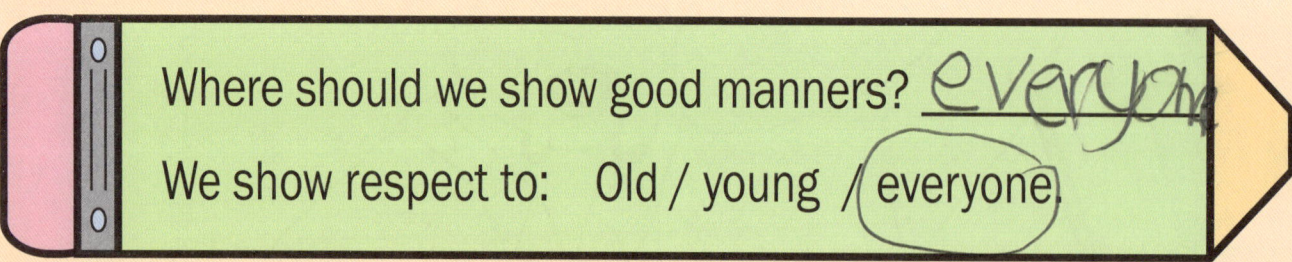

Where should we show good manners? _everyone_

We show respect to: Old / young / (everyone)

At school, we talk **politely** to our teachers and other students. We take care of all the books, chairs and tables. To be mean to others is being a **bully**. Allah does not like bullies.

We should have good manners in the masjid. We should not break anything in the masjid. When the **Imam** talks, we should be quiet and listen carefully. It is not nice to run around in the masjid. Making noise inside the masjid is not good manners.

During wudu, we should not **spill** water everywhere. During salat, we do not talk or laugh. We show respect to the Qur'an, and when Prophet's name is taken.

When someone is speaking, we should wait for our turn. Only when a person is done speaking, we can speak. It is not good manner if everybody speaks out at the same time. Snatching something from others is not good manners. If we want something, we should ask for it.

We should show good manners everywhere —at home, at school and outside. Even in the playground, we should have good manners. Pushing or shoving others is not good. When we have good manners in the playground, everyone can have fun. Everyone will be safe.

At home we should show good manners.   True / False

During salat we should not speak to others.   True / False

Words that I learned today:
Behave • Greeting • Politely • Bully • Imam • Spill

Homework
Weekend 21

1. Circle the picture that shows good manners while eating.

2. Circle the choices that show good manners.

While eating, where should our food be?

(a) On the plate.
(b) On our clothes.
(c) On the floor.

When you see the Imam, what do you say?

(a) Hello!
(b) Assalamu alaikum!
(c) Hi!

When someone visits you, what should you say?

(a) Go back.
(b) Please come in!
(c) You again?

3. Mark with ✓ if it is a good manners, mark with ✗ if it is not good manners.

When people pray in the masjid, we may scream and run around.

During wudu, we spill water on other people's clothes.

When the Imam is talking, we listen carefully.

During salat, we may tickle the person next to us.

In the class, we all talk at the same time.

We take good care of our books, chairs and tables.

Classwork
Weekend 22

Kindness and Sharing

Assalamu alaikum. Welcome to the class. These two friends have one small toy today. They are sharing it. Can you please color them?

We are kind when we help others. A kind person is not mean to others. When someone is in **difficulty** and we **treat** them nicely, we are kind.

Allah is very kind. Allah is kind to people, animals, birds, plants, and everything. Allah is **Rahman**, which means He is very Kind.

Our dear Prophet Muhammad (S) was a very kind person. He helped the Muslims. He helped the **non–Muslims** too to become good people. He was also kind to those who did not like him.

We should be kind to our families and friends. Our parents are kind and loving to us. When we talk nicely to others, we are kind. If we help our parents, we are kind to them. We are kind when we talk nicely to someone who is hurt.

We are kind when we **share** our things with others. When we share things, we may get it back. It is also OK if we do not get our things back. When we share our toys with others, we get a chance to play with our friends. When we get a chance, we should give away our toys to children who do not have toys. When we share, Allah loves us.

Allah is kind with birds, animals, plants. True / False

Prophet (S) was kind with non-Muslims. True / False

Allah tells us to share our food with others. He also tells us to share our money with others who do not have enough money. These are zakah and **sadaqah**. When we share our food and money with others, Allah gives us more. Shaitan scares us that if we give money we will become poor. We never become poor by giving out sadaqah.

Giving sadaqah will make us poor.   True / False

When we share, Allah gives us more.   True / False

Our Prophet (S) said if you smile at others it is a sadaqah. If someone is sad, we should try to make them smile. When we share our happiness, we are kind.

Now that we are done with our lesson, let us write something that we shared with others yesterday. Write down on the pencil the thing that you shared.

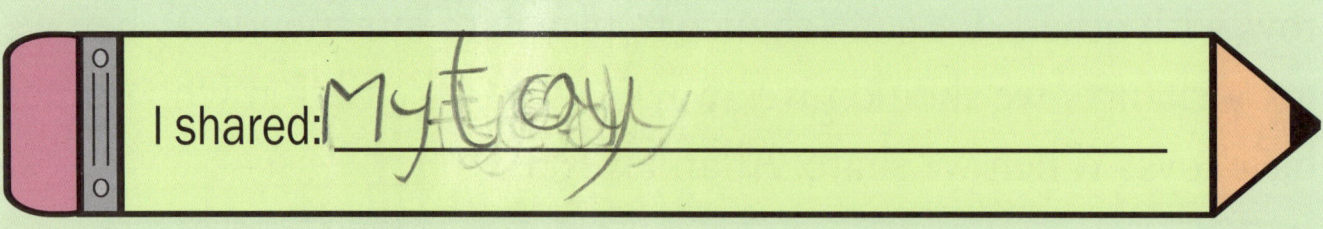

I shared: My toy

Words that I learned today:

Difficulty • Treat • Rahman • Non-Muslims • Share • Sadaqah

Homework
Weekend 22

1. Circle all the right choices. Allah is very Kind to:

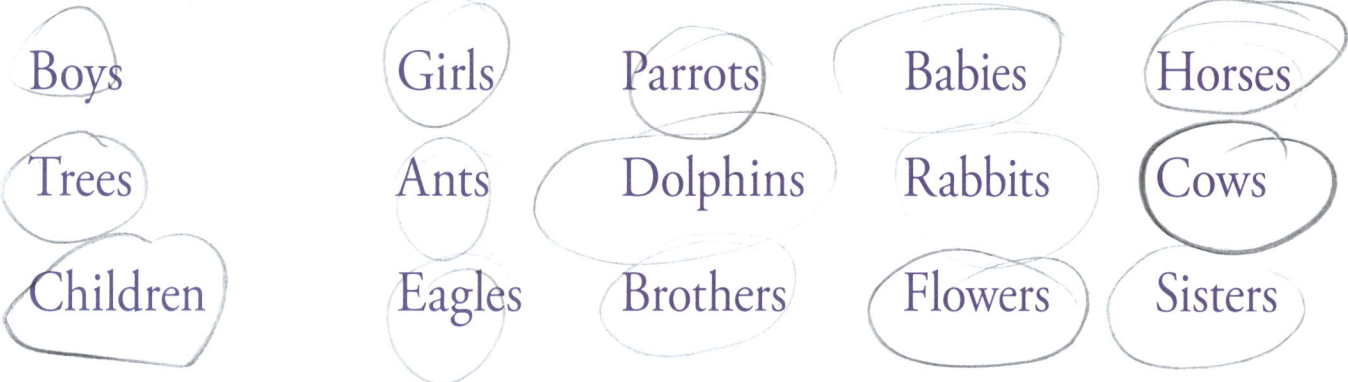

2. Rahman is a name of Allah. What does it mean?

_____

3. Mark the people with a ✓ if we have to be kind to them.

Mark the people with a ✗ if we do not have to be kind to them.

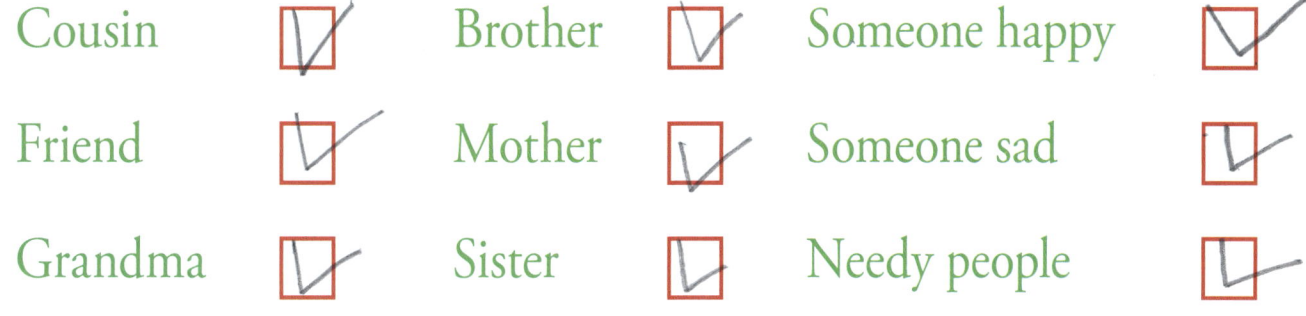

4. Circle the things that you may have and the things that you are willing to give away and share with needy children.

Things that I have

Things I may give away and share with needy children

Allah Rewards Good Work

Classwork
Weekend 23

Assalamu alaikum. Welcome to the class. Let us color Hanif and his **discovery** from under the bed.

Hanif is cleaning the **clutter** in his room. Under his bed, he found his favorite story book that was lost. Under the pile of coloring papers were his crayons. Hanif now knows that cleaning the room is a good work, as his **reward** was finding the lost storybook and the crayons.

Any time we do good work, Allah gives us rewards. Some rewards come early, some rewards come late. We get some rewards in this world. We will get some rewards in Heaven. Sometimes we get reward but we do not know it was a reward. Always the reward is better and bigger than the work.

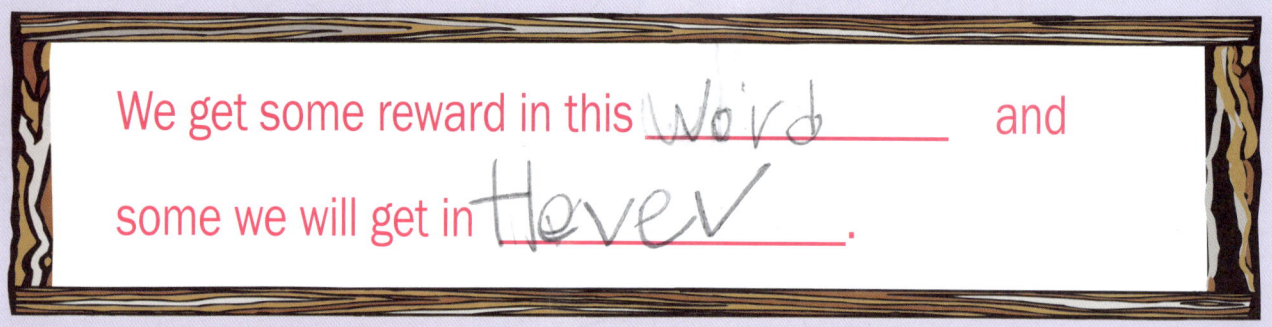

We get some reward in this ___word___ and some we will get in ___Hever___.

We can count some rewards such as money, gifts, clothes and toys. We cannot count some rewards, such as happiness and peace.

When we do something good for our family, everyone is happy. Happiness is the reward. When we work hard in school, the reward is good **grades**. When we get good grades, we are happy. Again, happiness is a reward.

When we make salat, give charity, or fast in Ramadan, Allah rewards us with peace and happiness is this world. He will also reward us in Heaven.

The Qur'an tells us to remind each other to do good work. The Qur'an also tells us to stop bad work of others. A good Muslim always tries to do good work. Everyday we get many chances to do good work. We should make use of these chances.

Keeping our classroom or the masjid clean is good work. Cleaning up after your game is good work. Doing your homework on time is good work. Talking nicely to others is good work. Can you think of other ways to do good work? Write down on the pencil one good work that you would like to do.

One good work that I would like to do is: _____

Words that I learned today:
Discovery • Clutter • Reward • Grade

Homework
Weekend 23

1. Mark with a ✓ if it will bring good rewards.

   Mark with a ✗ if it will not bring good rewards.

   Help the needy people.

   Keep the masjid clean.

   Keep your desk clean.

   Wear dirty clothes.

   Drop juice on the carpet.

   Make a dua to Allah.

   Get up early for Fajr salat.

2. Circle the works that bring good rewards, cross out works that will not bring good rewards.

   (Give your mother a hug.)   (Do Maghrib salat.)

   Break the pencils.   Eat rotten food.

   Waste food.   (Do homework on time.)

   (Listen to your teacher.)   Run around in the masjid.

3. Cross out the pictures that do not look like good work.

Respect

Classwork Weekend 24

Assalamu alaikum. Welcome to the class. Let us color this person who is reading the Qur'an with respect.

Respect is treating others the way we want to be treated. We show respect to others when we treat them nicely. Being mean, yelling or screaming at others is not a sign of respect.

When we show respect to others, people show respect to us. We speak politely to our elders. This is a sign of respect. We listen to others carefully. It is not respectful to start talking when others are talking. We also show respect to those who are younger to us. We should not yell at others. You should not pick your nose in front of others or stick out your tongue or make faces at others.

When we talk about Allah (swt), we should show respect. Saying "*Subhana-hu wa ta'ala*" after Allah's name is showing respect to Him.

When we talk about the Prophet, we say "*Sallal-lahu alai hi wa sallam*" after his name. These words show our respect to Muhammad (S). We do not make any bad comments about Rasulullah (S). In this book whenever you see (S), remember to say *Sallal-lahu alai hi wa sallam*.

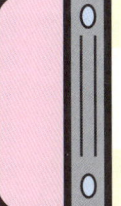

We need not show respect to children.	True / False
We show respect to Allah and Rasul.	True / False

We read the Qur'an with respect. We touch the Qur'an with clean hands. We never put the Qur'an in a dirty place. When someone **recites** the Qur'an, we show respect by listening quietly.

We show respect to our **property**. We also show respect to other people's properties. We should not destroy things for fun. We do not take other people's things without asking them first. We show respect to our friends and neighbors.

We should also respect ourselves. This means we take good care of our body and mind. When we get up, study, eat and sleep on time, we are showing respect to us. Wearing clean clothes shows we respect ourselves.

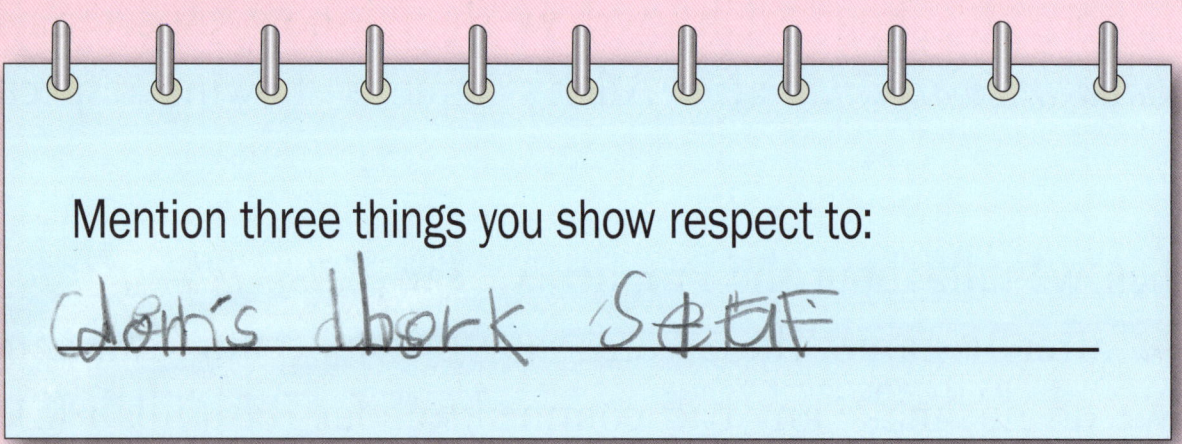

Mention three things you show respect to:
cloths work self

Words that I learned today:

Subhana-hu wa ta'ala • Sallal-lahu alai hi wa sallam •
Recite • Property

Homework
Weekend 24

1. Circle the ways you can show respect. Cross out the bad actions.

   Talking when the teacher is talking.

   Keeping your books in good shape.

   Fooling around when someone is praying.

   Helping your mother carry the groceries.

   Listening when someone is speaking.

   Writing on the wall with a crayon.

   Being kind to the poor.

   Shutting down the door on someone.

2. Your mother is cleaning the kitchen. What should you do to show respect? (Circle the correct answer)

   (a) Run through the kitchen with dirty feet.

   (b) Get the cleaning supplies for her.

   (c) Drop toys all over the kitchen.

Your sister is studying for an important test. What should you do to show respect?

(a) Be quiet when you are near her.

(b) Keep on bothering her.

(c) Play loudly near her.

Your mother is praying. What do you do to show respect?

(a) Run around her.

(b) Talk and shout.

(c) Be quiet.

3. Circle the people you should show respect to:

Brother	Cashier	Mother	Postal worker
Father	Teacher	Cousin	Muhammad (S)
Prophets	Plumber	Doctor	Construction worker
Nurse	Sister	Imam	Uncle	Aunt

Classwork

Weekend 25

Forgiveness

Assalamu alaikum. Welcome to the class. Let us start by coloring this picture. Someone is mean and someone is sad. Color the mean boy blue, and color the sad boy with many colors to cheer him up.

A long time ago, many people of Makkah were mean to Rasulullah (S). They gave a hard time to all the Muslims. Rasulullah (S) could not live in Makkah anymore. He and many Muslims went to Madinah to save their lives. When he was in Madinah, people from Makkah came and fought against the Muslims. One day, Rasulullah (S) came back to Makkah. He came with many **soldiers**. The people of Makkah were scared. They thought Rasulullah (S) would **punish** them. But Rasulullah (S) was kind. He forgave all the people. Forgiveness is to treat others nicely even if others are not nice to you. People of Makkah were so happy, they became Muslim.

After returning to Makkah Rasulullah (S) ____fofa____ the people.

Then the people in Makkah became ____muslims____

Ibrahim (A) was a great prophet. He told everyone to be good Muslim. His father would not listen to him. His father was **rude** to him. His father threw him out of his home. Ibrahim (A) was sad that his father would not become a Muslim. His father was mean, but Ibrahim (A) was not. He asked Allah (swt) to forgive his father.

Which prophet had a rude father? ____Ibrahim____

We should practice forgiveness everyday. When someone is mean to us, we should not be mean. We should tell them that it is not good to be mean. Forgiveness does not mean we are **afraid**. We can forgive when we are strong. When we forgive others, Allah rewards us.

Sometimes, we do things that are not good. Allah becomes unhappy at our bad work. If we say sorry, then Allah forgives us. After that, we should not do the same bad thing again.

As we want Allah to forgive us, we should also forgive others.

If we forgive others, what does Allah give us? _reward_

If we say sorry, Allah will _forgive_ us.

Words that I learned today:

Forgiveness • Soldiers • Punish • Rude • Afraid

Homework Weekend 25

1. Circle **C** if it is correct, **W** if it is wrong.

   Forgiveness should be done on Fridays only. ~~C~~ **W**

   Forgiveness means we are afraid. ~~C~~ **W**

   Strong people can forgive others. **C** W

   Rasulullah (S) did not forgive anyone. C **W**

   If we say sorry, Allah forgives us. **C** W

   Circle the correct choice in questions 2, 3, 4 and 5.

2. Rasulullah (S) forgave the people of Makkah when he came back to:

   (a) **Makkah**.
   (b) Madinah.
   (c) Cairo.

3. Ibrahim (A) was kind, and asked Allah to forgave his:

   (a) Soldiers.
   (b) **Father**.
   (c) Prophet.

4. When someone is mean to us, we should:

   (a) Say thank you.
   (b) Be mean with them.
   (c) Not be mean with them.

5. If we make a mistake and say sorry to Allah, then we should:

   (a) Not do the mistake again.
   (b) Forget about it.
   (c) Keep doing the same mistake.

6. Fill in the blanks with the right word from the box:

   | sorry | Muslims | strong | home |

   When Rasulullah (S) forgave the people of Makkah, they happily became ___Muslims___.

   If we do something bad, we should say ___sorry___ to Allah.

   Ibrahim (A)'s father threw him out from his ___home___.

   A ___strong___ person should forgive others.

Classwork
Weekend 26

Love of Allah

Assalamu alaikum. As Allah loves us so much, He gave us many beautiful things, such as flowers. Can you color this flower?

If you make something nice or draw a nice picture, you start to like it. Allah made this world and everything in it. He also made all the stars and **planets**. He made all of these in a very nice way. He loves all his creations.

One of Allah's beautiful names is **al-Wadud**. The name means the Loving One. He loves us much more than we can imagine.

Allah is so loving that He is **Rahman**. It is one of His names. It means He is very Kind. He prepared many things for His creations. Allah knows that we will need air, water, sunshine and many other things. Since He loves us so much He gave us all these even before we were born.

Allah is **Rahim**. This is one of His beautiful names. It means Rewarding. If we do a small good work, He gives us a large reward.

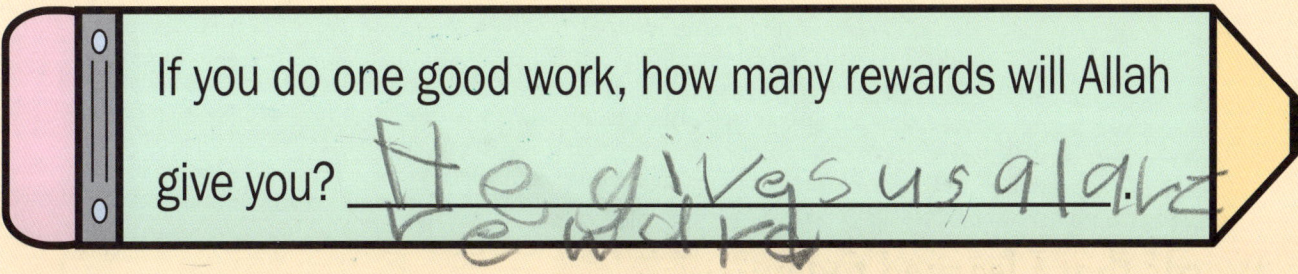

If you do one good work, how many rewards will Allah give you? _He gives us a large reward_

If you make a toy car with blocks, and it does not run nicely, you fix it. You fix your toy car, because you love it. People are Allah's creation. Sometimes people do bad things. Allah wants the bad people become good again. Therefore He punishes them. **Punishment** is also Allah's way of showing His love and affection. Some people learn from the punishment and become good. If some people do not become good, they will be punished more in the Hereafter.

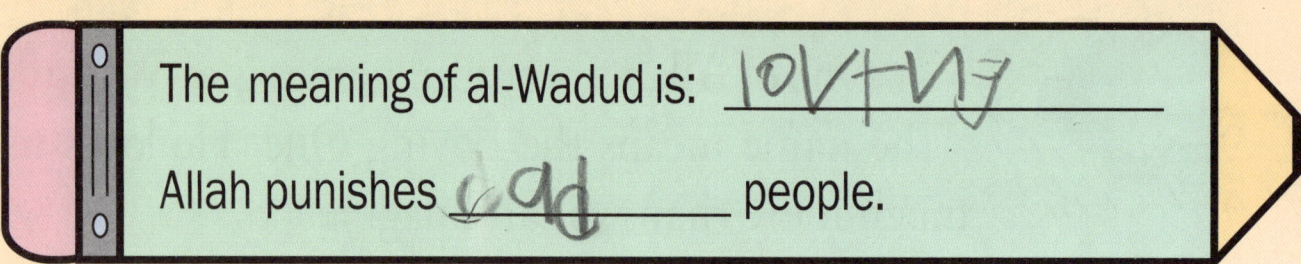

The meaning of al-Wadud is: loving

Allah punishes bad people.

Allah sent the Qur'an to show us the right path. If the Qur'an was not there, we would be lost. Allah also sent Muhammad (S) to guide us. All these show how much Allah loves us. He listens to us all the time. If we make a **dua** to Allah, He listens to it.

Every good thing that we do is because of Allah's love. He loves us more than anyone else.

Words that I learned today:

Planets • Wadud • Rahman • Rahim • Punishment • Dua

Homework Weekend 26

1. Write **Yes** if Allah will love us, and write **No** if Allah will not love us for doing these works.

Make Salah on time. _Yes_

Be nice to our dad and mom. _Yes_

Be mean to our friends. _No_

Not help people in need. _No_

Listen to our teachers. _Yes_

Make a dua to Allah. _Yes_

2. Circle the words which remind us about the Love of Allah for us.

Family   Air   Mountain   Trees   Milk

Sunlight   River   Mother   Teacher   Water

Prophet   Grass   Flower   Fruits   Snow

3. Circle **C** if it is correct, **W** if it is wrong.

Allah punishes bad people so that they may become good people. (C) W

Allah loves us, so He listens to our dua. (C) W

Allah loves us, so He rewards us. (C) W

Allah forgets to reward some good work. (C) W

Eid: *Two Festivals*

Classwork Weekend 27

Assalamu alaikum. Welcome to the class. Let us color these two friends who are greeting each other on the day of Eid.

Every year we have two Eid. These are days of festivals. Festival means days of happiness. In Arabic, Eid means happiness.

Eid al-Fitr comes on the day after the fasting of Ramadan ends. We fast for one month in Ramadan. On the day of Eid, we do not fast. We visit the homes of friends and families. We enjoy good food and thank Allah for all His blessings. We wear clean clothes. We share our happiness. On the day of Eid-al Fitr we give charity called **Zakat al-Fitr** to the needy people. This is a day of happiness for all Muslims, rich and poor.

After which month Eid al-Fitr comes? _____

What charity do we give on the day of Eid? _____

Another Eid is **Eid al-Adha**. This Eid comes at the end of Hajj. Hajj is done in Makkah. In Hajj, people remember Prophet Ibrahim (A) in many ways. People who do not go for Hajj remember the prophet by doing a **sacrifice** on Eid-al Adha. On this Eid, we sacrifice an animal. We share the meat with our friends, families and also the needy. Everybody enjoys on the day of Eid.

In which Eid do we sacrifice an animal? _____

Which Eid is done after Hajj? _____

On the mornings of Eid days, we go for a prayer in a large place. People from all over the city come to this salat. Before the salat, we recite **takbirat**. We listen to a **khutbah** or speech by the Imam. The khutbah has many good advice.

We meet our friends and families, we hug them and greet them saying "**Eid Mubarak**."

Words that I learned today:

Eid-al Fitr • Zakat al-Fitr • Eid al-Adha • Sacrifice • Takbirat • Khutbah • Eid Mubarak

Homework
Weekend
27

1. Mark with ✓ if it is correct, mark with ✗ if it is wrong.

   Eid-al Fitr is at the end of Ramadan. ☐

   Eid-al Fitr is at the end of Hajj. ☐

   Eid-al Adha is at the end of Hajj. ☐

   On Eid-al Fitr, we sacrifice an animal. ☐

2. Cross out the things that are not done in Eid.

   Prayer   Fighting   Fun

   Happiness   Fasting   Sharing

3. Write a list of four things that you want to get on Eid day.

   _____

   _____

   _____

   _____

4. Write a list of two things that you want to share with others on Eid Day.

_____

_____

5. Write a list of homes you want to visit, and the list of people that you want to come to your home on the day of Eid.

I want to go to the homes of:	I want these people to come to our home:
_____	_____
_____	_____
_____	_____
_____	_____
_____	_____

Thanking Allah

Classwork
Weekend 28

Assalamu alaikum. We can thank Allah in many ways. Being in **Sujud** is a way to say thanks to Allah. Can you color this boy who is thanking Allah?

Every day we say thanks to people for many reasons. We say 'thank you' when people give us something. We say 'thank you' when people do something good for us. If we do not say *thank you*, it makes us look bad. It makes us look **proud**. Allah does not like proud people. Pride is a sign of Shaitan.

Allah gives us all things that we need in the world. He gave us air, water, sun, moon, green earth, plants, animals, vegetables, rivers, and oceans for our benefit. He gave us ear, nose, lips, hands and all the body parts. Should we not say "**Thank You, Allah**" for all His blessings? If we do not give thanks to Allah, we behave like Shaitan. Allah does not like people who do not give thanks.

We should thank to Allah for everything He gave us. Name any three things for which we should say thanks.

dogs   _cats_   _Familys_

We have many ways to thank Allah. We can say **Shukr Allah** whenever any good thing happens to us. So many good things happen to us all the time that we cannot really count them.

Making **salat** is a good way to thank Allah every day. We start the day by thanking Allah, by praying Fajr salat. During the day, we say "thank you" to Allah by making other salat. We end our day by saying another thanks to Allah, by making Isha salat.

We also thank Allah by **fasting**. Fasting reminds us to thank Allah for all the things and food that we have. On the day of **Eid al-Fitr**, we again say thanks to Allah for Ramadan and all the food that we get over the year. **Eid al-Adha** is a time to thank Allah for our friends and families, and to remember that our family belongs to Allah.

When we give **Zakah**, we also thank Allah for all the things and wealth that He gave us.

Rasulullah (S) used to thank Allah all the time. We should also thank Allah all the time.

Words that I learned today:
Sujud • Proud • Shukr Allah

Homework Weekend 28

1. Write three different ways that you can thank Allah.

   Fasting   Sifkih

   fasting

   Zakah

2. How should we start our day?

   by

3. How should we end our day?

   by

4. Now that you have finished reading all the lessons in this book, what should you say to Allah?

   _____

Test Your Knowledge - 1

(All questions are based on the lessons taught in the book)

1. What is the first pillar of Islam?

2. Name all the pillars of Islam.

3. When we do salat, which direction do we face?

4. What is the language of the Qur'an?

5. Which angel brought the Qur'an to Rasulullah (S)?

6. What was the name of the father of Prophet Muhammad (S)?

7. What was the name of the mother of Prophet Muhammad (S)?

8. What is the name of the first prophet in Islam?

9. What is the name of the last prophet in Islam?

10. What is the name of the religion Allah gave us?

11. What are the five daily salat for a Muslim?

12. Before doing salat, someone loudly declares prayer call. What is the name of the call?

Answer:
1. Shahadah 2. Shahadah, Salat, Fasting, Zakah and Hajj 3. Towards Ka'bah
4. Arabic 5. Jibril 6. Abdullah 7. Aminah
8. Adam (A) 9. Muhammad (S) 10. Islam
11. Fajr, Dhuhur, Asr, Maghrib and Isha 12. Adhan

Test Your Knowledge - 2

(All questions are based on the lessons taught in the book)

1. Who whispers bad things in our mind?

2. Before doing salat we clean ourselves with water. What is the name of the cleaning?

3. In which month do we fast?

4. What is the name of the meal people eat to break their fast?

5. At the end of Ramadan we celebrate. What is the name of the celebration?

6. Who can get the zakat money we pay?

7. During Hajj, we remember the teachings of a prophet. Which prophet do we remember?

8. During Hajj men wear a special cloth. What is the color of the cloth?

9. What is the name of the special cloth men wear during Hajj?

10. What is the name of the book Allah sent to prophet Isa (A)?

11. What is the name of a chapter in the Qur'an?

12. How long did it take to complete the Qur'an?

Answer:
1. Shaitan 2. Wudu 3. Ramadan 4. Iftar
5. Eid al-Fitr 6. The needy people 7. Ibrahim (A) 8. White
9. Ihram 10. Injil 11. Surah 12. 23 years

Outline of Curriculum – Grades 1, 2 and 3

Every year the curriculum begins with a few topics on Allāh, the Qur'ān, the Prophet (S), the Hadīth or Sunnah. In the early years the emphasis is given on the 5-pillars, but each year the emphasis increases. Every year history of some of the prophets is introduced in an age appropriate manner. Each year, several lessons are devoted to Islamic values to make the children grow up with good understanding of Islamic manners, values and morals. All the lessons are followed by homework.

Week	1st Grade	2nd Grade	3rd Grade
1	Allāh	Allāh the Creator	What does Allāh do
2	Islam	Blessings of Allāh	Some names of Allāh
3	Our Faith	The Qur'ān	Allāh : the Merciful
4	Muhammad (S)	Muhammad (S)	Allāh : the Judge
5	Qur'ān	Sunnah and Hadīth	We are Muslims
6	Exam is recommended in this week		
7	5 pillars of Islam	5 pillars of Islam	Other names of the Qur'ān
8	Shahādah	Shahādah	Hadīth
9	Salāt and Wudū	Salāt	Shahādah
10	Fasting	Sawm	Types of salāt
11	Zakah	Charity	Why to do salāt
12	Exam is recommended in this week		
13	Hajj	Hajj	Sawm
14	Saying bismillāh	Wudū	Charity
15	Angels	Four khalīfas	Hajj
16	Shaitān	Ibrāhīm (A)	Prophet (S) in Makkah
17	Adam (A)	Ya'qūb (A) and Yūsuf (A)	Prophet (S) in Madinah
18	Nūh (A)	Mūsā (A) and Harun (A)	How Rasul (S) treated others
19	Exam is recommended in this week		
20	Ibrāhīm (A)	Yūnus (A)	Ismā'īl (A) and Ishāq (A)
21	Mūsā (A)	Angels	Dāwūd (A)
22	'Isā (A)	Foods that we may eat	'Isā (A)
23	Makkah and Madinah	Truthfulness	Being kind
24	Good manners	Kindness	Forgiveness
25	Kindness and sharing	Respect	Good deeds
26	Exam is recommended in this week		
27	Allāh rewards good works	Responsibility	Cleanliness
28	Respect	Obedience	Right Path
29	Forgiveness	Cleanliness	Muslim family
30	Love of Allāh	Honesty	Perseverance
31	Eid	Day of Judgment and Hereafter	Punctuality
32	Thanking Allāh	Muslims from different nations	Jinn
33	Exam is recommended in this week		

Outline of Curriculum – Grades 4, 5 and 6

By 5th grade a summarized biography of the Prophet (S) is completed with an understanding of events that shaped his life and early Islam. By 6th grade, the students will have studied the biography of most of the prominent prophets at least once. By now the students will have learned all the fundamental principles and all key concepts of Islam. Even if the students do not come back to weekend schools after 6th grade, still they will have gained significant age-appropriate knowledge about Islam.

Week	4th Grade	5th Grade	6th Grade
1	Rewards of Allāh	Allāh our sole Master	Attributes of Allāh
2	Discipline of Allāh	Why should we worship Allāh	Promise of Allāh
3	Some names of Allāh	Revelation of the Qur'ān	Objective of the Qur'ān
4	Books of Allāh	Characteristics of prophets	Compilation of the Qur'ān
5	Pre-Islamic Arabia	Battle of Badr	Previous Scriptures and the Qur'ān
6	Exam is recommended in this week		
7	The Year of the Elephant	Battle of Uhud	Importance of Shahādah
8	Early life of Muhammad (S)	Battle of Trench	Hadīth, compilation, narrators
9	Life before prophethood	Hudaibiyah Treaty	Nūh (A)
10	Receipt of prophethood	Conquest of Makkah	Talut, Jalut and Dāwūd (A)
11	Makkan period	Adam (A)	Dāwūd (A) and Sulaimān (A)
12	Exam is recommended in this week		
13	Pledges of Aqaba	Ibrāhīm (A) and his arguments	Sulaimān (A) and Queen of Saba
14	Hijrat to Madinah	Ibrāhīm (A) and idols	Mūsā (A) and Fir'awn
15	Madīnan period	Luqmān (A) and his teachings	Israelites after their rescue
16	Victory of Makkah	Yūsuf (A) – Childhood and life in Aziz's home	Mūsā (A) and Khidir
17	Abū Bakr (R)	Yūsuf (A) – life in prison and his dream interpretation	'Isā (A) and Maryam (ra)
18	'Umar al-Khattāb (R)	Yūsuf (A) - dream fulfills	Khadījah (ra)
19	Exam is recommended in this week		
20	'Uthmān ibn 'Affan (R)	Ayyūb (A)	'A'ishah (ra)
21	'Ali Ibn Abu Tālib (R)	Zakariyyāh (A) and Yahyā (A)	Fātimah (ra)
22	Compilers of Hadīth	Maryam	Awakening
23	Shaitān's mode of action	Major Masjid in the World	Rūh and Nafs
24	Hūd (A)	Upholding truth	Angel and Jinn
25	Sālih (A)	Responsibility and Punctuality	Shaitān's strategy
26	Exam is recommended in this week		
27	Mūsā (A)	My mind, my body	Taqwā
28	Sulaimān (A)	Kindness and forgiveness	My friend is Muslim now
29	Truthfulness	Middle Path	Friendship with others / with opposite gender
30	Perseverance	Significance of salāt	Reading salāt vs performing salāt
31	Day of Judgment	Significance of fasting	Muslims around the world
32	'Eid and its significance	Zakāt and sadaqah - significance	People of other faith
33	Exam is recommended in this week		

Outline of Curriculum – Grades 7, 8 and 9

Application of knowledge is gradually emphasized through carefully selected topics. Details about some of the prophets are introduced to highlight the abiding moral in their lives. In 8th grade several battles and early Muslims' struggle are discussed in detail. Depth and emphasis in the lessons require increased attention from the students. Age appropriate moral lessons e.g. gossip, friendship, peer pressure, dating, indecency, enjoining good and forbidding evil, etc. are covered.

Week	7th Grade	8th Grade	9th Grade
1	Why Islam, what is Islam	Divine Names	Signs of Allāh in nature
2	The Qur'ān - other names	Objective of the Qur'ān	Ponder over the Qur'ān
3	Seeking forgiveness of Allah - Istighfar	Hadīth	Preservation & compilation of the Qur'ān
4	Allāh: Angry or Kind	Madhhab	Ibadat - some easy ways to do it
5	Islamic Greetings	Hope, hopefulness, hopelessness	Why human being are superior
6	Exam is recommended in this week		
7	Adam (A)	Trial	Is Islam a violent religion
8	'Ad and Thamūd	Friends and friendship	Peer pressure
9	Stories of Ibrāhīm (A)-I	Friendship with Non-Muslims	Choices We make
10	Stories of Ibrāhīm (A) -II	Dating in Islam	Dating in Islam
11	Sacrifice of Ibrāhīm (A)	Duties towards Parents	Alcohol and gambling
12	Exam is recommended in this week		
13	Lūt (A)	Islam for Middle School Student	Permitted & prohibited food
14	Yūsuf (A)- Story of overcoming temptation	Battle of Badr	Food of the People of the Book
15	Dwellers of Cave	Battle of Uhud	Khadījah (ra)
16	Dhul Qurnain	Banu Qaynuka	Prophet's multiple marriages
17	Abū Sufyān	Banu Nadir	Marriage with Zainab (ra)
18	Khālid Ibn Walīd (R)	Battle of Khandaq	The Prophet - a great army general
19	Exam is recommended in this week		
20	How to Achieve Success	Banu Qurayzah	God's chosen people
21	Character of the prophets	Surah Al-Ahzab on Battle of Khandaq	Mūsā's Personality
22	Prophet's marriages	Hudaibiyah Treaty	Prophecy of Muhammad(S) in Bible
23	Purification	Tabūk Expedition	Shī'ah Muslims
24	Permitted and prohibited	Farewell Pilgrimage	Muslims in North America
25	Lailatul Qadr	Performance of Hajj	Life cycle of truth
26	Exam is recommended in this week		
27	Fasting in Ramadan	Paradise and Hell	How Ramadan makes us better
28	My family is Muslim now	Finality of Prophethood	Indecency
29	Amr bil ma'rūf	Origin and history of Shī'ah	Allegations against the Prophet (S)
30	Guard your tongue	Ummayad Dynasty	Family values
31	Lessons from past civilizations	Abbasid Dynasty	Shariah
32	Science in the Qur'ān	Permitted and prohibited food	Justice in Islam
33	Exam is recommended in this week		

Outline of Curriculum – Grades 10, 11 and 12

In 10th, 11th and 12th grades, the topics increasingly prepare the youths to tune their young-adult life. More serious issues are introduced that have real life implications. Application of knowledge continues to be emphasized. Age appropriate moral lessons like righteousness in Islam, marriage, dowry issues, divorce process, jihad etc. are introduced.

Week	10th Grade	11th Grade	12th Grade
1	History of Allāh	"Discovering" God	Our God, their God
2	An analysis of Fātiha	Kalam of Allāh	Loving Allāh
3	Fātiha vs. Lord's Prayer	Precedence of mercy in Allāh	Literal interpretation of the Qur'ān
4	Muhkam Mutashabihat verses	Importance of the Qur'ān in life	Management 101 - from the Prophet's life
5	Being Khalifa on Earth	Succession to Muhammad (S)	Apostasy
6	Exam is recommended in this week		
7	False Piety	Victory comes from apparent setback	Husband and wife - garment for each other
8	The Bible and the Qur'ān	Accountability	Dowry process
9	Adam and Eve in the Garden	Righteousness in Islam	Divorce process
10	Ten Commandments and Islam	10 years of Life changing foundation	Lian verses
11	Racism in Islam	Light upon the Light	Hijab verses
12	Exam is recommended in this week		
13	Superstition	Ruh, Nafs, Spirit, Bodies	Marital relations of the Prophet (S)
14	Al-Asr - Timing of the Day	Responsibilities in Married Life	Men are head of household
15	Position of Women in Islam	Divorce	Flogging an adulterer
16	Marriage with Non-Muslims	Balancing faith amid diversity	Why two women witness
17	Distinctive Females in Qur'ān	Importance of keeping the "trust"	Hur in Heaven
18	Women's Rights in Islam	Music in Islam	Is Islam a violent religion
19	Exam is recommended in this week		
20	Establishing Salat- Institutionalize it	Fitra - Innate human nature	Jihad verses
21	Goodly Loan	Heedlessness in human being	Hajj - understanding the significance
22	Fiqh	Importance of tolerance	"Beating thy wife"
23	Death	Guidance and misguidance	"Part time Muslim"
24	Do not Transgress Limits	Stages of life and death	Muslim youths in the US
25	Public Finance in Early Islam	This world and next world	MSA - An introduction
26	Exam is recommended in this week		
27	Business Ethics	How to enjoy life Islamic way	Islamophobia - how to deal with it
28	Balance in Life	Wrongdoings - how to identify and avoid them	Future Muslims
29	Secular and Religious Duties	How to pray Janaza prayer	Independent project
30	Islam in India	Understanding Judaism	Independent project
31	Islam in Spain	Judaism, Christianity and Islam	Independent project
32	Islam in Turkey	Dependence, independence	Independent project
33	Exam is recommended in this week		

Other useful books from weekendLearning

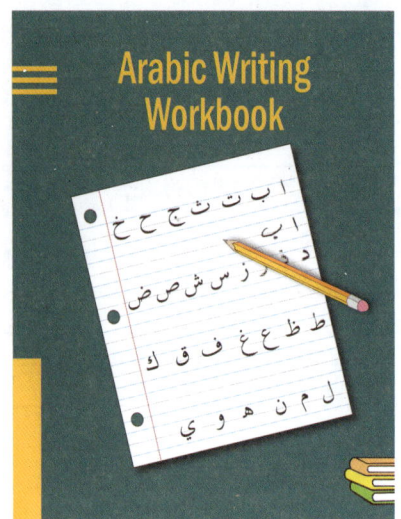

Arabic Writing Workbook

96 pages $10.00

Teach students how to write Arabic with easy to follow instructions. Practice alphabets come with grey and dotted letters, followed by blank lines to polish writing skills. Plenty of pages for year long practice writing.

21 Du'ā for Children: Supplications from Al-Qur'ān

By Mansur Ahmad

28 pages $2.00

Allāh wants us to always make du'ā to Him for everything. The finest du'ā are those taught by Allāh in the Qur'ān. Use this booklet to teach 21 finest du'ā and many more. Give one copy to each student in your school. It is a life long companion and a great learning tool.

Quiz Book on Islam for All Levels of Expertise (2nd ed.)

By Husain A. Nuri

160 pages $10.00

Written by Quiz Master of an Interstate Quiz Bowl. The book is designed to boost Islamic knowledge of children. Even adults will enjoy the book. The book has over 1,700 questions covering more than 100 different topics. The questions are divided into basic, intermediate and advanced sections. Each page has about 15–17 questions. Many questions have explanatory answers. Turn to this book to quickly learn variety of facts about Islam.

Juz 'Amma for School Students

By Husain A. Nuri and Mansur Ahmad

216 pages $12.00

The book is a student friendly presentation of the 30th Part of the Qur'an. The book contains large and clear Arabic text, transliteration and translation in three-column format. Each sūrah starts with an introduction, followed by explanation of the verses. A "word to know" section provides root and derivatives of several key words. This is followed by a word-to-word meaning of the entire sūrah. Each chapter ends with some teachings in the sūrah that the children can apply in their everyday lifves. A short question section reinforces the materials learned.